Earth Science

S0-BZY-581

Table of Contents

A Scientist's Equipment

Name _____

Label the equipment below.

Word Bank

beaker	ringstand	graduated cylinder
test tube	funnel	dropper
thermometer	flask	test tube holder
Bunsen burner	alcohol lamp	

How Long Is It?

Name _____

The meter is the standard unit of measurement when measuring
the length of an object or the distance between two objects.
Use either **kilometer, meter, centimeter** or **millimeter** to label
the unit that would be used to measure the objects pictured.

Word Bank

meter   kilometer   centimeter   millimeter

The Long and Short of It

Name _____

Weight, length, area and volume are properties of matter that scientists can measure. Scientists use the units of grams, meters and liters to measure these properties.

Write the abbreviation for each of these units of measurement.

Unit of Measure	Abbreviation
gram	
kilogram	
milligram	
meter	
kilometer	
centimeter	
millimeter	
square centimeters	
cubic centimeters	
liter	
milliliter	

Word Bank

g	kg	mg	m	km	cm
mm	cm^2	cm^3	l	ml	

Celsius vs. Fahrenheit

Name _____

The thermometer on this page compares the Celsius and Fahrenheit scales. Label the temperatures on the Celsius and Fahrenheit scales.

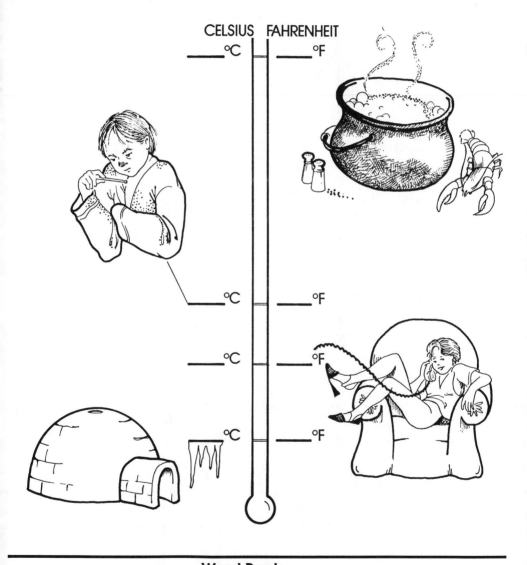

Word Bank

0	20	32	37
98.6	100	212	70

Reading a Graduated Cylinder

Name _____

Small quantities of a liquid can be measured using a graduated cylinder. You may notice how the liquid curves up the side of the cylinder. To get an accurate reading, read the measurement at the bottom of the curve, or *meniscus*. Read these volumes.

1. _____ ml

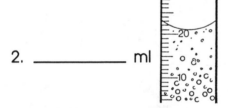

2. _____ ml

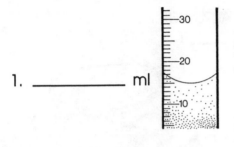

3. _____ ml

4. _____ ml

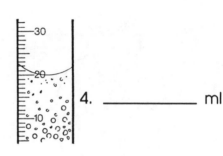

5. _____ ml

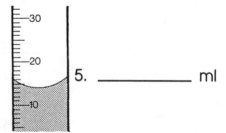

6. _____ ml

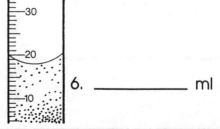

Chemical Symbols

Name _____

Use the symbols to find the names of the elements needed to complete the puzzle.

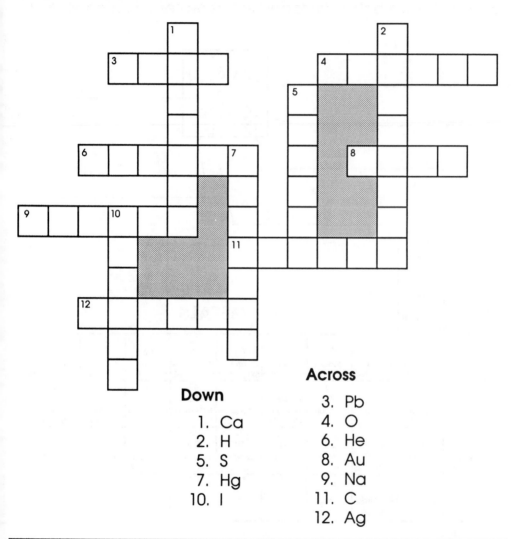

Down

1. Ca
2. H
5. S
7. Hg
10. I

Across

3. Pb
4. O
6. He
8. Au
9. Na
11. C
12. Ag

Word Bank

lead	carbon	sulfur
sodium	mercury	gold
calcium	helium	iodine
oxygen	silver	hydrogen

   IF0227 Earth Science

Periodic Table of Elements

Name _____

The periodic table can give you a lot of information about each of the elements. Use the Word Bank to label the type of information that the symbols, names and letters represent for an element.

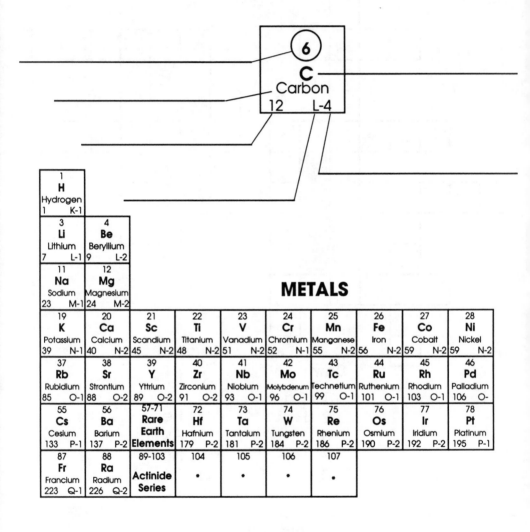

Word Bank

atomic number   element's symbol   electrons in outer shell

atomic mass   element's name   outer electron shell

Atoms

Name _____

Label the parts of the helium atom pictured.

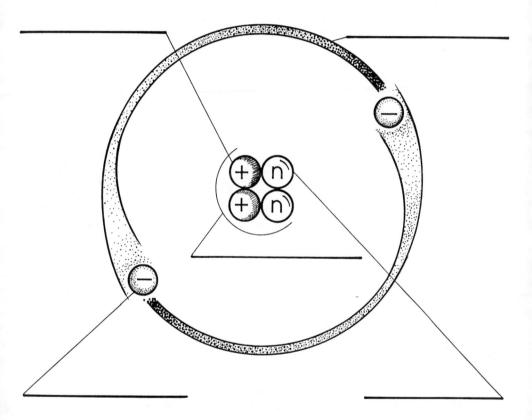

Word Bank

proton	nucleus	electron
orbit (shell)	neutron	

Name That Molecule!

Name _____

Write the chemical formula for each molecule pictured.

_____   _____   _____

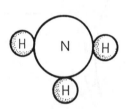 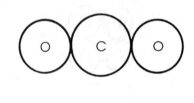 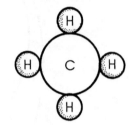

_____   _____   _____

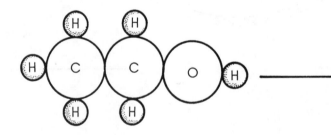 _____

Word Bank

H_2O CH_4 H_2S Fe_2O_3
C_2H_5OH CO_2 NH_3

Chemical Formulas

Name _____

A chemical formula is a shorthand way to write the name of a compound. Complete the chart below for each of the formulas.

	Compound	Formula	Elements
1.		NaCl	
2.		HCl	
3.		NaOH	
4.		H_2O	
5.		CO_2	
6.		H_2SO_4	
7.		$CuSO_4$	
8.		C_2H_5OH	

Word Bank

sodium chloride
water
sulfuric acid
sodium
copper

hydrochloric acid
oxygen
copper sulfate
chlorine
sulfur

sodium hydroxide
carbon dioxide
alcohol
hydrogen
carbon

Dry Cells

Name _____

The dry cell is a source of portable power used in flashlights, toys, and radios. There are three basic kinds of dry cells that are commonly used – carbon-zinc, alkaline, and mercury.

Label the parts of this carbon-zinc dry cell illustration.

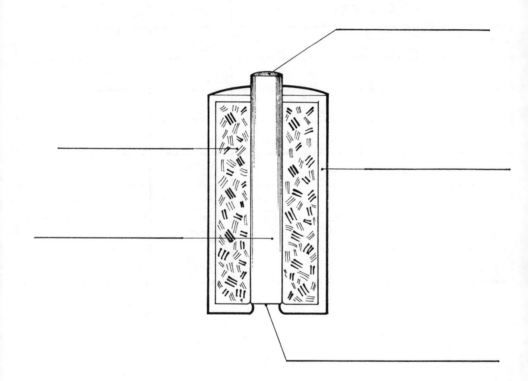

Word Bank

positive terminal	zinc container	chemical paste
negative terminal	carbon rod	

Light Bulb

Name _____

Label the parts of the incandescent light bulb pictured below.

Word Bank

bulb	filaments	contact
glass support	connecting and supporting wires	base

Drawing Electrical Circuits

Name _____

There are three types of simple electrical circuits: a closed circuit, a parallel circuit, and a series circuit. Each type can be set up in more than one way.

Draw lines to show where the wires should connect to make these circuits.

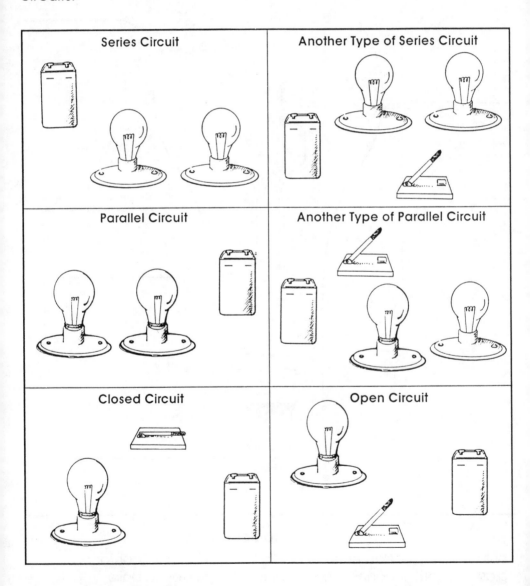

Series Circuit	Another Type of Series Circuit
Parallel Circuit	Another Type of Parallel Circuit
Closed Circuit	Open Circuit

Classy Levers

Name _____

Three classes of levers are pictured below. Label each class of lever and the three lever parts.

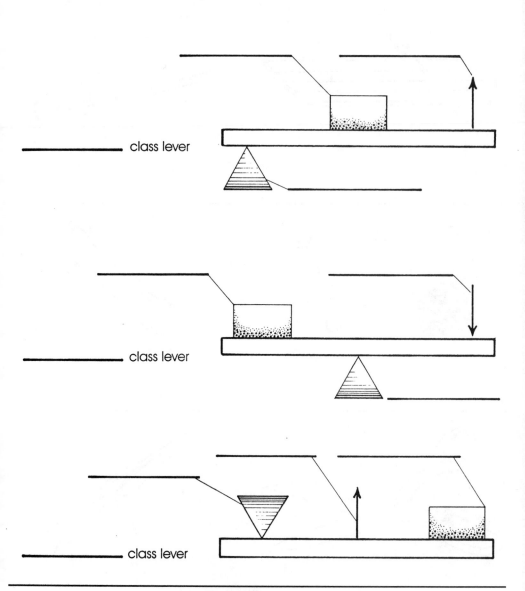

_____ class lever

_____ class lever

_____ class lever

Word Bank

first	second	third
load	force	fulcrum

Practical Levers

Name _____

In the space under each picture below write **first, second** or **third** to tell the class of the lever.

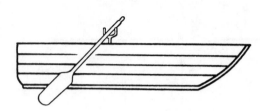

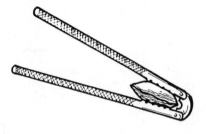

_____ _____

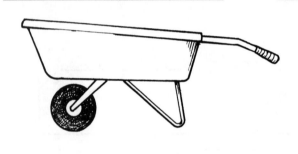

_____ _____

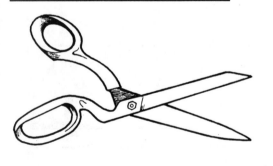

_____ _____

Special Inclined Planes

Name _____

Some simple machines are pictured below. Some of these simple machines are special inclined planes, called wedges and screws. Put an **X** on the simple machines that are not special inclined planes. Label the special inclined planes either **screw** or **wedge**.

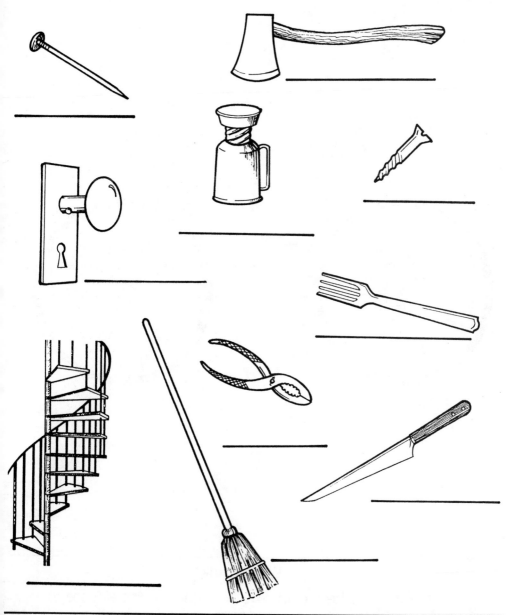

Pedal Power

Name _____

Your bicycle is a combination of many simple machines. Study the bicycle on this page. Circle and label as many simple machines that you can find on the bicycle shown.

Word Bank

lever   wheel and axle   inclined plane (screw)

The Seasons

Name _____

The diagram below shows the Earth's position in its orbit on four
different dates. On the solid line label the equinox dates. On the
dotted lines name the season for the Northern hemisphere.

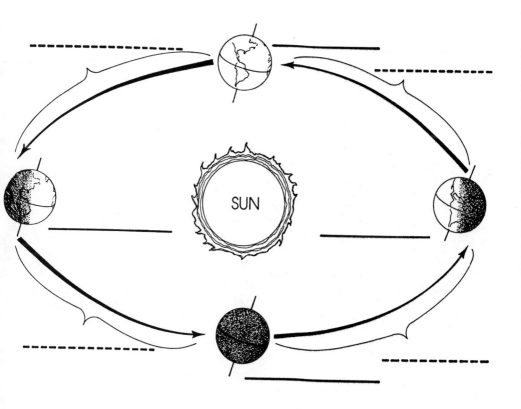

Word Bank

March 21	December 22	spring	fall
September 22	June 21	winter	summer

Summer and Winter

Name _____

The illustration below shows the Earth's position in relation to the Sun for the summer and winter in the Northern Hemisphere. Label the seasons for the Northern Hemisphere, and name the imaginary lines of latitude on the Earth.

Word Bank

summer   Antarctic Circle   Equator
Arctic Circle   Tropic of Cancer   winter
Tropic of Capricorn

Day and Night

Name _____

Day and night are the result of the Earth's rotation on its axis.
Label the illustration below.

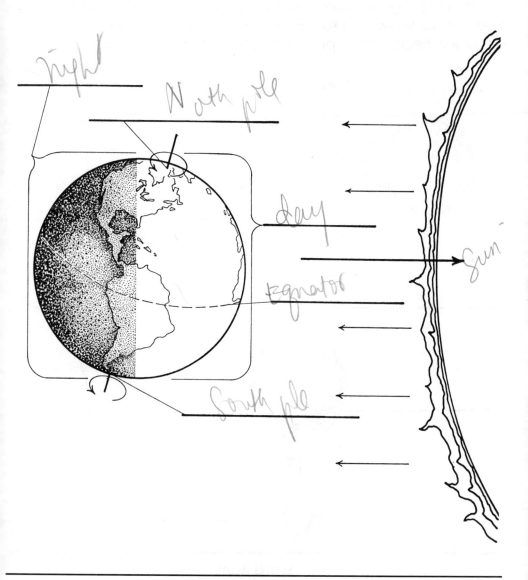

Handwritten labels: night · North pole · day · Equator · South pole · sun

---

Word Bank

North Pole	Equator	day
South Pole	night	sun

High Tide

Name _____

The ocean tides are caused mostly by the moon's gravity. When the Sun, moon and Earth line up, the gravitational pull is greatest causing the highest tides, the spring tides. The lowest tides, neap tides, occur when the sun, Earth and moon form right angles. Label the neap tides, spring tides, sun, Earth and moon.

_____ tides

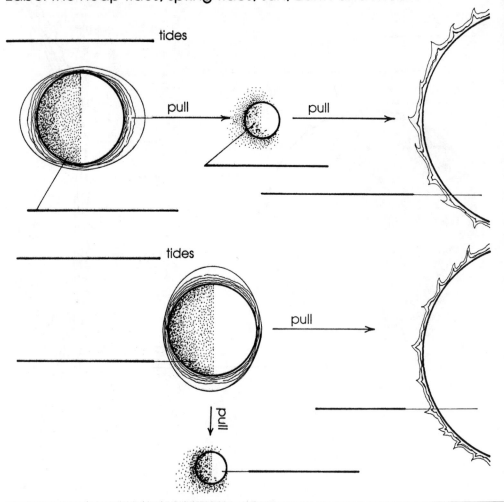

_____ tides

Word Bank

neap tides   Earth
moon   sun
spring tides

Earth Shadow

Name _____

When the sun, Earth and moon are in direct line, the moon moves into the Earth's shadow causing a **lunar eclipse**. Label the orbits and bodies in the illustration below.

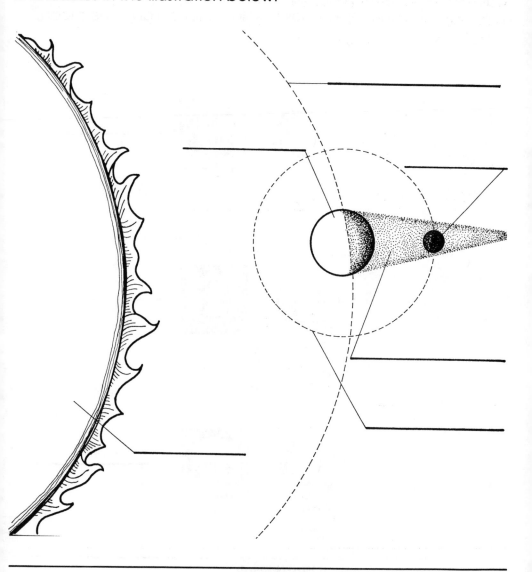

Word Bank

Earth orbit	moon	moon orbit
Earth	sun	Earth's shadow

 IF0227 Earth Science

Moon Shadows

Name _____

When the moon is directly between the Earth and the sun, an eclipse of the sun occurs. The type of **solar eclipse** that occurs depends on how much sunlight the moon blocks from the view on Earth. Label the three kinds of solar eclipse. Label the moon, sun and Earth.

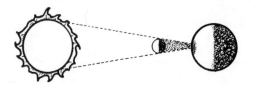 _____

 _____

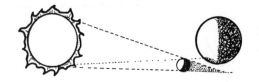 _____

Word Bank

total eclipse	moon
sun	partial eclipse
annular eclipse	Earth

 IF0227 Earth Science

Changing Faces

Name _____

As the moon revolves around the Earth, we can see different amounts of the moon's lighted part. Study the drawing of the moon's different phases and each phase as it would be seen from the Earth. Label each phase.

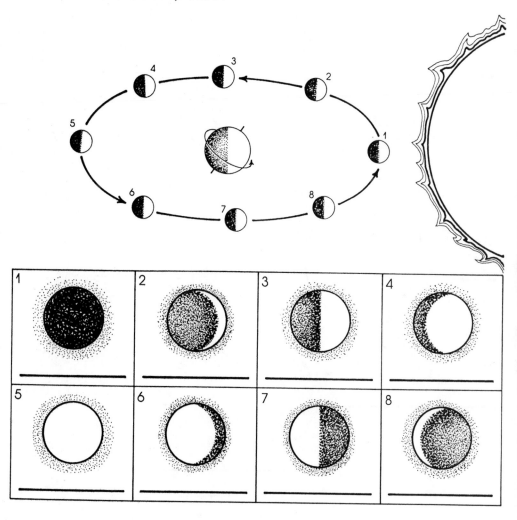

Word Bank

new moon	waxing crescent	first quarter
waxing gibbous	full moon	waning gibbous
last quarter	waning crescent	

Waning and Waxing Moon

Name _____

Label the different phases of the moon.

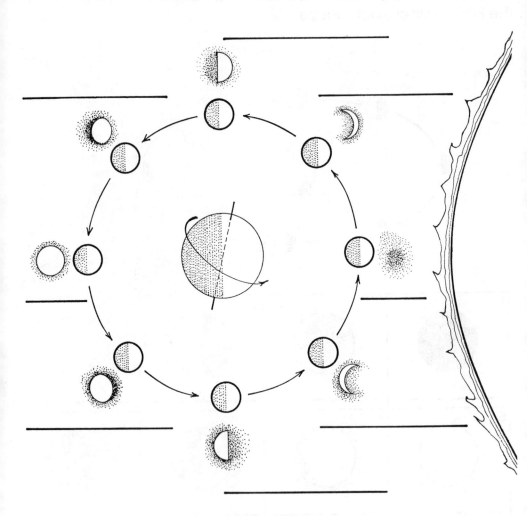

_____

_____   _____

_____   _____

_____   _____

Word Bank

new   last quarter   first quarter
full   waxing crescent   waning gibbous
waxing gibbous   waning crescent

The Inner Planets

Name _____

The planets that are closest to the sun are called the Inner Planets. Label the Inner Planets and the sun.

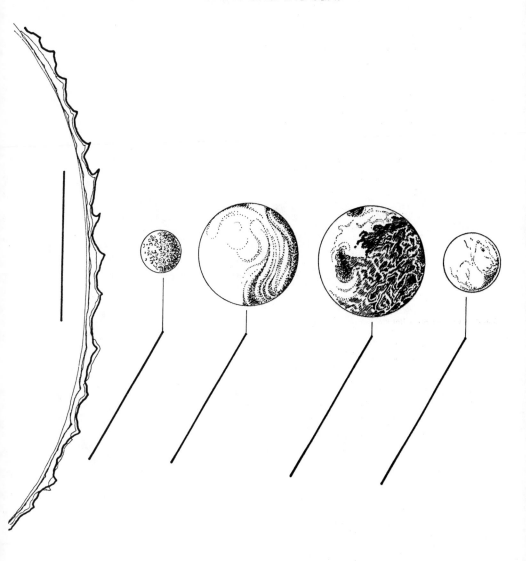

Word Bank

sun   Venus   Mercury
Earth   Mars

The Outer Planets

Name _____

The planets that are farthest from the sun are called the Outer Planets. Label the Outer Planets.

Sun
and
Inner
Planets ←

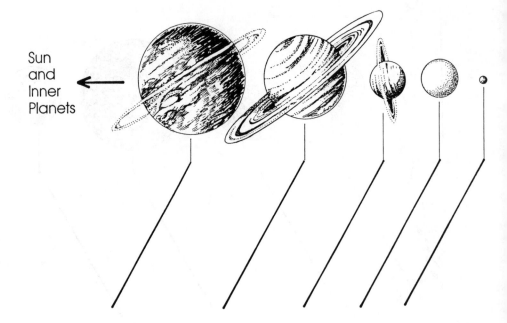

Word Bank

Jupiter   Saturn   Uranus
Neptune   Pluto

Exploring Our Solar System

Name _____

Comets, asteroids, and some meteors travel around the sun in our solar system. But the largest objects traveling around the sun are the planets. Use your science book, encyclopedia, or another source to complete the chart about the planets of our solar system.

Planet	Position From the Sun	Revolution Time (Length of Year – Earth Days)	Rotation Time	Distance From the Sun

Fill in the names of the planets where they belong.

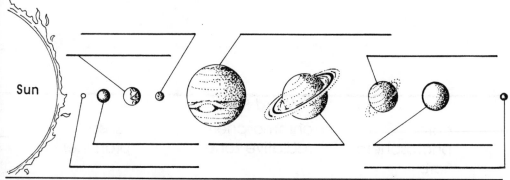

Sun

Our Closest Star – the Sun

Name _____

The sun is the closest star to the Earth. Label the different layers and features of the sun.

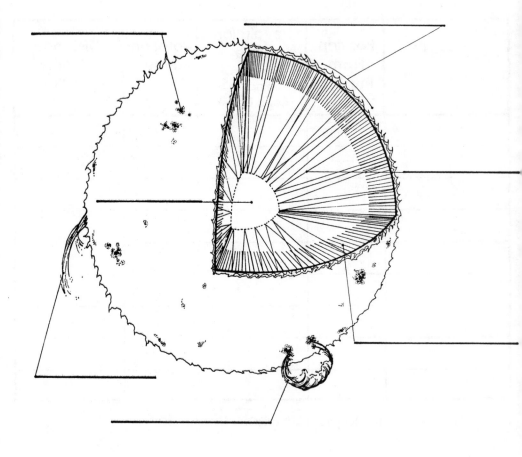

Word Bank

core	chromosphere	sunspot
photosphere	radiative zone	prominence
flare		

Dirty Snowballs

Name _____

Comets are like "dirty snowballs." Label the parts of these frozen masses of gas and dust particles.

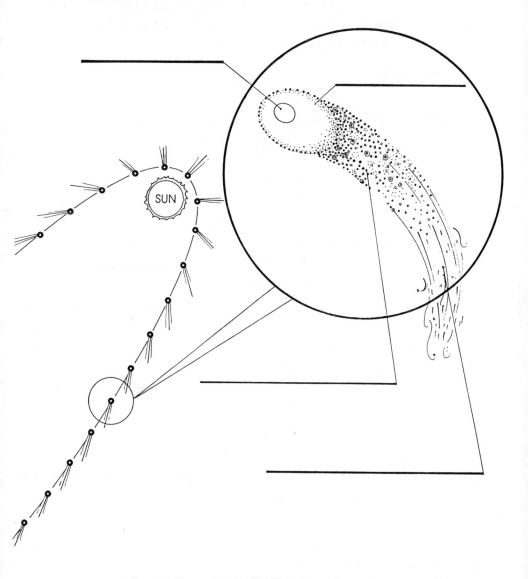

Word Bank

nucleus   coma   gas tail   dust tail

The Asteroid Belt

Name _____

Scientists believe that asteroids may be pieces of a planet that was torn apart millions of years ago. Thousands of large astroids have been tracked, but hundreds of thousands of smaller asteroids are in the asteroid belt. Label the asteroid belt and the planets in the illustration below.

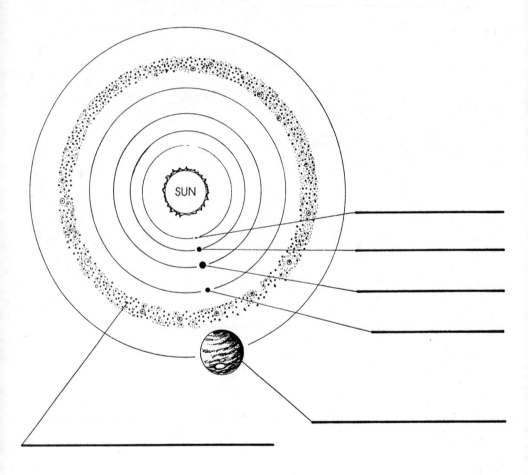

Word Bank

| Mercury | Venus | Earth |
| Mars | Jupiter | asteroid belt |

The North Star

Name _____

Because the Earth rotates, all the stars in the sky appear to move from east to west. Because Polaris is directly above the North Pole it does not move, and so it is also called the North Star.

Polaris is found in the constellation Ursa Minor, also called the Little Dipper. The Big Dipper is found in the constellation Ursa Major, also called the Great Bear. Trace the Big Dipper and Little Dipper. Label Polaris.

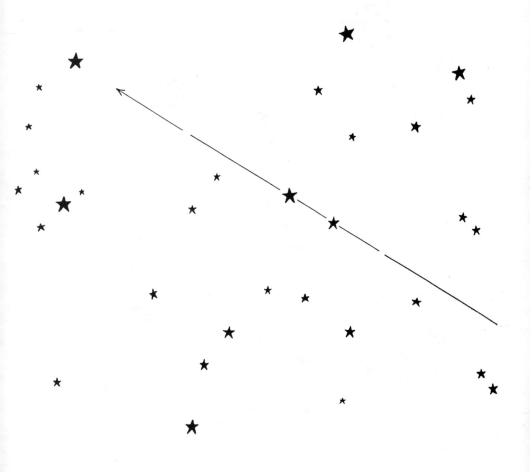

Word Bank

Big Dipper   Little Dipper   Polaris

Pictures in the Night Sky

Name _____

For thousands of years people from every culture have gazed into the night sky and imagined groups of stars outlining a picture. These star pictures, called **constellations**, are like giant dot-to-dot puzzles in the night sky.

Name these well-known constellations.

_____

_____

_____

_____

_____

_____

Word Bank

Orion	Cygnus	Leo
Scorpio	Taurus	Cassiopeia

"Optic Glass"

Name _____

In 1609 the Italian astronomer, Galileo, was the first person to see the heavenly bodies closer than they really were with his "optic glass," or telescope. Label the refractor and reflector telescopes and their parts.

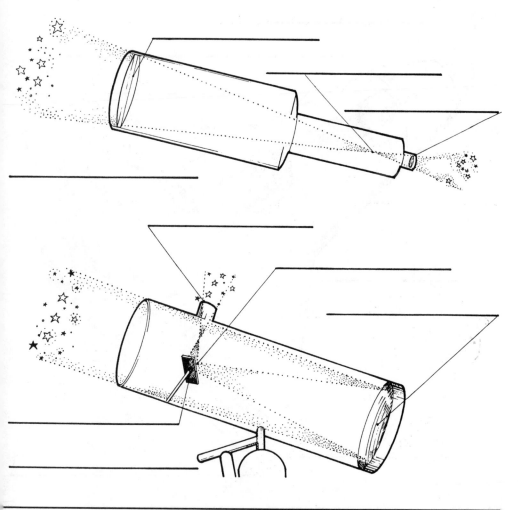

Word Bank

reflector telescope   refractor telescope
objective lens   eyepiece lens
focal point   flat mirror
objective mirror

The Space Shuttle

Name _____

Label the parts of the Space Shuttle.

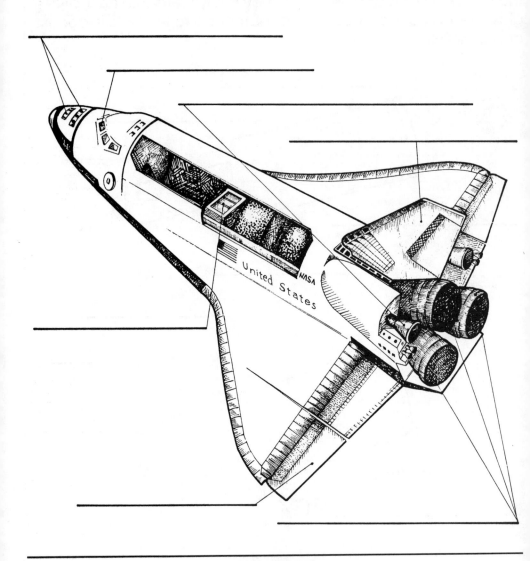

Word Bank

payload bay
cockpit
elevon
main engines

rudder and speed brake
reaction control jets
orbital maneuvering system engine

Answer Key
Earth Science

A Scientist's Equipment

Name _____

Label the equipment below.

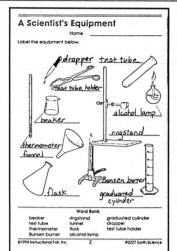

dropper · test tube · test tube holder · alcohol lamp · beaker · ringstand · thermometer · funnel · Bunsen burner · graduated cylinder · flask

How Long Is It?

Name _____

The meter is the standard unit of measurement when measuring the length of an object or the distance between two objects. Use either kilometer, meter, centimeter or millimeter to label the unit that would be used to measure the objects pictured.

kilometer · meter · millimeter · centimeter · centimeter · millimeter · centimeter · meter

The Long and Short of It

Name _____

Weight, length, area and volume are properties of matter that scientists can measure. Scientists use the units of grams, meters and liters to measure these properties.

Write the abbreviation for each of these units of measurement.

Unit of Measure	Abbreviation
gram	g
kilogram	kg
milligram	mg
meter	m
kilometer	km
centimeter	cm
millimeter	mm
square centimeters	cm^2
cubic centimeters	cm^3
liter	l
milliliter	ml

Celsius vs. Fahrenheit

Name _____

The thermometer on this page compares the Celsius and Fahrenheit scales. Label the temperatures on the Celsius and Fahrenheit scales.

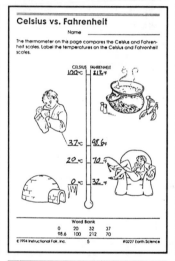

CELSIUS FAHRENHEIT
100 °C   212 °F
37 °C   98.6 °F
20 °C   70 °F
0 °C   32 °F

Reading a Graduated Cylinder

Name _____

Small quantities of a liquid can be measured using a graduated cylinder. You may notice how the liquid curves up the side of the cylinder. To get an accurate reading, read the measurement at the bottom of the curve, or meniscus. Read these volumes.

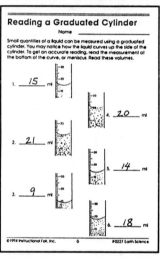

1. 15 ml
2. 21 ml
3. 9 ml
4. 20 ml
5. 14 ml
6. 18 ml

Chemical Symbols

Name _____

Use the symbols to find the names of the elements needed to complete the puzzle.

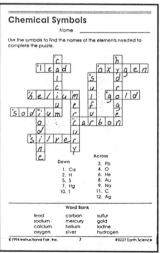

Down
1. Ca
2. H
5. S
7. Hg
10. I

Across
3. Pb
4. O
6. He
8. Au
9. Na
11. C
12. Ag

Periodic Table of Elements

Name _____

The periodic table can give you a lot of information about each of the elements. Use the Word Bank to label the type of information that the symbols, names and letters represent for an element.

atomic number · element's name · atomic mass · outer electron shell · element's symbol · electrons in outer shell

METALS

Atoms

Name _____

Label the parts of the helium atom pictured.

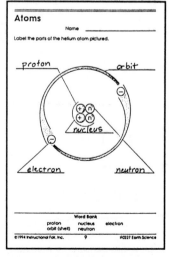

proton · orbit · electron · nucleus · neutron

Name That Molecule!

Name _____

Write the chemical formula for each molecule pictured.

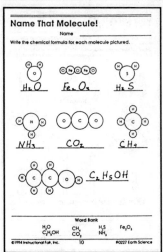

H_2O Fe_2O_3 H_2S

NH_3 CO_2 CH_4

C_2H_5OH

Chemical Formulas

Name _____

A chemical formula is a shorthand way to write the name of a compound. Complete the chart below for each of the formulas.

	Compound	Formula	Elements
1	sodium chloride	NaCl	sodium, chlorine
2	hydrochloric acid	HCl	hydrogen, chlorine
3	sodium hydroxide	NaOH	sodium, hydrogen, oxygen
4	water	H_2O	hydrogen, oxygen
5	carbon dioxide	CO_2	carbon, oxygen
6	sulfuric acid	H_2SO_4	hydrogen, sulfur, oxygen
7	copper sulfate	$CuSO_4$	copper, sulfur, oxygen
8	alcohol	C_2H_5OH	carbon, hydrogen, oxygen

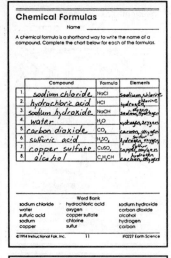

Dry Cells

Name _____

The dry cell is a source of portable power used in flashlights, toys, and radios. There are three basic kinds of dry cells that are commonly used – carbon-zinc, alkaline, and mercury.

Label the parts of this carbon-zinc dry cell illustration.

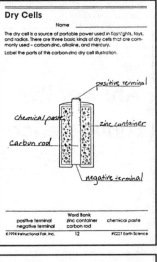

positive terminal
zinc container
chemical paste
carbon rod
negative terminal

Light Bulb

Name _____

Label the parts of the incandescent light bulb pictured below.

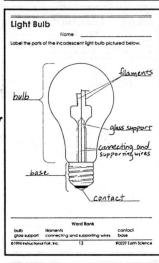

filaments
bulb
glass support
connecting and supporting wires
base
contact

Drawing Electrical Circuits

Name _____

There are three types of simple electrical circuits: a closed circuit, a parallel circuit, and a series circuit. Each type can be set up in more than one way.

Draw lines to show where the wires should connect to make these circuits.

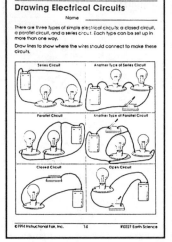

Classy Levers

Name _____

Three classes of levers are pictured below. Label each class of lever and the three lever parts.

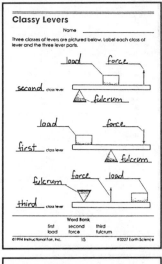

load   force
second class lever   fulcrum
load   force
first class lever   fulcrum
fulcrum   force   load
third class lever

Practical Levers

Name _____

In the space under each picture below write first, second or third to tell the class of the lever.

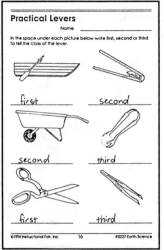

first   second
second   third
first   third

©1994 Instructional Fair, Inc.   16   IF0227 Earth Science

Special Inclined Planes

Name _____

Some simple machines are pictured below. Some of these simple machines are special inclined planes, called wedges and screws. Put an X on the simple machines that are not special inclined planes. Label the special inclined planes either screw or wedge.

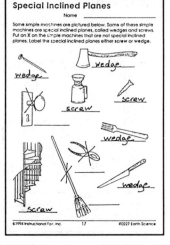

wedge
wedge
screw
screw
wedge
wedge
screw

©1994 Instructional Fair, Inc.   17   IF0227 Earth Science

Pedal Power

Name _____

Your bicycle is a combination of many simple machines. Study the bicycle on this page. Circle and label as many simple machines that you can find on the bicycle shown.

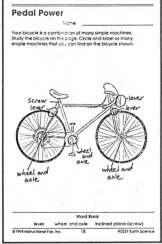

screw
lever
lever
lever
wheel and axle
wheel and axle
wheel and axle

The Seasons

Name

The diagram below shows the Earth's position in its orbit on four different dates. On the solid line label the equinox dates. On the dotted lines name the season for the Northern hemisphere.

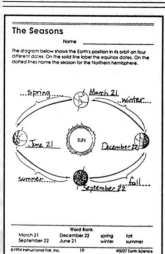

	Word Bank		
March 21	December 22	spring	fall
September 22	June 21	winter	summer

©1994 Instructional Fair, Inc. 19 IF0227 Earth Science

Summer and Winter

Name

The illustration below shows the Earth's position in relation to the Sun for the summer and winter in the Northern Hemisphere. Label the seasons for the Northern Hemisphere, and name the imaginary lines of latitude on the Earth.

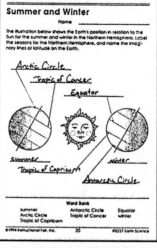

	Word Bank	
summer	Antarctic Circle	Equator
Arctic Circle	Tropic of Cancer	winter
Tropic of Capricorn		

©1994 Instructional Fair, Inc. 20 IF0227 Earth Science

Day and Night

Name

Day and night are the result of the Earth's rotation on its axis. Label the illustration below.

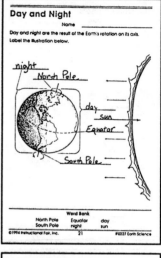

High Tide

Name

The ocean tides are caused mostly by the moon's gravity. When the Sun, moon and Earth line up, the gravitational pull is greatest causing the highest tides, the spring tides. The lowest tides, neap tides, occur when the sun, Earth and moon form right angles. Label the neap tides, spring tides, sun, Earth and moon.

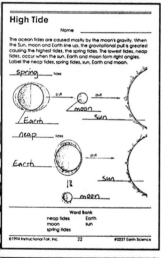

Earth Shadow

Name

When the sun, Earth and moon are in direct line, the moon moves into the Earth's shadow causing a lunar eclipse. Label the orbits and bodies in the illustration below.

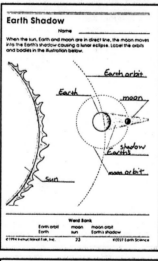

	Word Bank	
Earth orbit	moon	moon orbit
Earth	sun	Earth's shadow

©1994 Instructional Fair, Inc. 23 IF0227 Earth Science

Moon Shadows

Name

When the moon is directly between the Earth and the sun, an eclipse of the sun occurs. The type of solar eclipse that occurs depends on how much sunlight the moon blocks from the view on Earth. Label the three kinds of solar eclipse. Label the moon, sun and Earth.

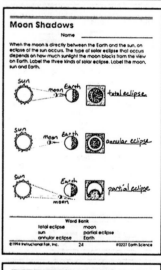

	Word Bank	
total eclipse	moon	
sun	partial eclipse	
annular eclipse	Earth	

©1994 Instructional Fair, Inc. 24 IF0227 Earth Science

Changing Faces

Name

As the moon revolves around the Earth, we can see different amounts of the moon's lighted part. Study the drawing of the moon's different phases and each phase as it would be seen from the Earth. Label each phase.

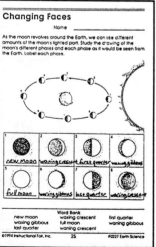

	Word Bank	
new moon	waxing crescent	first quarter
waxing gibbous	full moon	waning gibbous
last quarter	waning crescent	

©1994 Instructional Fair, Inc. 25 IF0227 Earth Science

Waning and Waxing Moon

Name

Label the different phases of the moon.

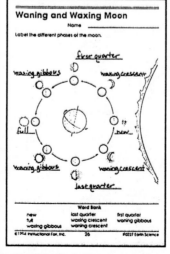

	Word Bank	
new	last quarter	first quarter
full	waxing crescent	waning gibbous
waxing gibbous	waning crescent	

©1994 Instructional Fair, Inc. 26 IF0227 Earth Science

The Inner Planets

Name

The planets that are closest to the sun are called the Inner Planets. Label the Inner Planets and the sun.

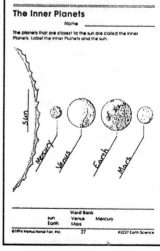

The Outer Planets

Name _____

The planets that are farthest from the sun are called the Outer Planets. Label the Outer Planets.

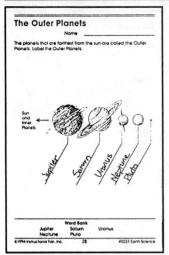

Sun and Inner Planets →

Jupiter Saturn Uranus Neptune Pluto

Word Bank
Jupiter Saturn Uranus
Neptune Pluto

©1994 Instructional Fair, Inc. 28 #0227 Earth Science

Exploring Our Solar System

Name _____

Comets, asteroids, and some meteors travel around the sun in our solar system. But the largest objects traveling around the sun are the planets. Use your science book, encyclopedia, or another source to complete the chart about the planets of our solar system.

Planet	Position From the Sun	Revolution Time (Length of Year = Earth Days)	Rotation Time	Distance From the Sun
Mercury	1st	88	59 days	36 million miles
Venus	2nd	225	243 days	67,230,000 miles
Earth	3rd	365	56 min.	93,000,000 miles
Mars	4th	687	24 hours 37 min.	141,700,000 miles
Jupiter	5th	4,333	9 hours 55 min.	483,700,000 miles
Saturn	6th	10,759	10 hours 39 min.	885,200,000 miles
Uranus	7th	30,685	16-28 hours	1,781 million miles
Neptune	8th	60,188	18-20 hours	2,788 million miles
Pluto	9th	90,700	6 days	3,660 million miles

Fill in the names of the planets where they belong.

Mars Earth Jupiter Uranus
Sun Venus Saturn Neptune Pluto
Mercury

©1994 Instructional Fair, Inc. 29 #0227 Earth Science

Our Closest Star – the Sun

Name _____

The sun is the closest star to the Earth. Label the different layers and features of the sun.

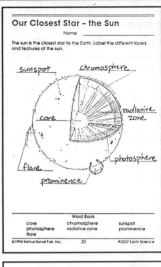

sunspot chromosphere
core radiative zone
flare photosphere
prominence

Word Bank
core chromosphere sunspot
photosphere radiative zone prominence
flare

©1994 Instructional Fair, Inc. 30 #0227 Earth Science

Dirty Snowballs

Name _____

Comets are like "dirty snowballs." Label the parts of these frozen masses of gas and dust particles.

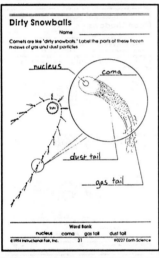

nucleus coma
dust tail
gas tail

Word Bank
nucleus coma gas tail dust tail

©1994 Instructional Fair, Inc. 31 #0227 Earth Science

The Asteroid Belt

Name _____

Scientists believe that asteroids may be pieces of a planet that was torn apart millions of years ago. Thousands of large asteroids have been tracked, but hundreds of thousands of smaller asteroids are in the asteroid belt. Label the asteroid belt and the planets in the illustration below.

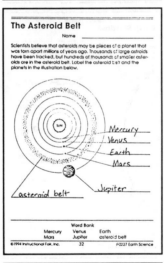

Mercury
Venus
Earth
Mars
asteroid belt Jupiter

Word Bank
Mercury Venus Earth
Mars Jupiter asteroid belt

©1994 Instructional Fair, Inc. 32 #0227 Earth Science

The North Star

Name _____

Because the Earth rotates, all the stars in the sky appear to move from east to west. Because Polaris is directly above the North Pole it does not move, and so it is also called the North Star.

Polaris is found in the constellation Ursa Minor, also called the Little Dipper. The Big Dipper is found in the constellation Ursa Major, also called the Great Bear. Trace the Big Dipper and Little Dipper. Label Polaris.

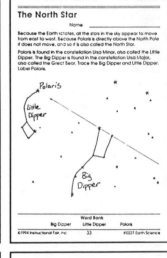

Polaris
Little Dipper
Big Dipper

Word Bank
Big Dipper Little Dipper Polaris

©1994 Instructional Fair, Inc. 33 #0227 Earth Science

Pictures in the Night Sky

Name _____

For thousands of years people from every culture have gazed into the night sky and imagined groups of stars outlining a picture. These star pictures, called constellations, are like giant dot-to-dot puzzles in the night sky.

Name these well-known constellations.

Leo
Scorpio
Cassiopeia
Orion Cygnus Taurus

Word Bank
Orion Cygnus Leo
Scorpio Taurus Cassiopeia

©1994 Instructional Fair, Inc. 34 #0227 Earth Science

"Optic Glass"

Name _____

In 1609 the Italian astronomer, Galileo, was the first person to see the heavenly bodies closer than they really were with his "optic glass," or telescope. Label the refractor and reflector telescopes and their parts.

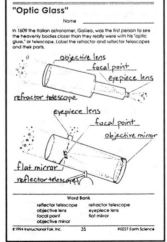

objective lens
focal point
eyepiece lens
refractor telescope
eyepiece lens
focal point
objective mirror
flat mirror
reflector telescope

Word Bank
reflector telescope refractor telescope
objective lens eyepiece lens
focal point flat mirror
objective mirror

©1994 Instructional Fair, Inc. 35 #0227 Earth Science

The Space Shuttle

Name _____

Label the parts of the Space Shuttle.

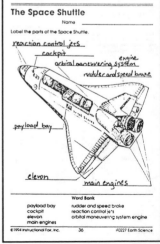

reaction control jets
cockpit
engine
orbital maneuvering system
rudder and speed brake
payload bay
elevon
main engines

Word Bank
payload bay rudder and speed brake
cockpit reaction control jets
elevon orbital maneuvering system engine
main engines

©1994 Instructional Fair, Inc. 36 #0227 Earth Science

©1994 Instructional Fair, Inc.

IF0227 Earth Science

Hemispheres

Name

The Earth is a giant sphere. When the Earth is divided into two equal parts, each part is called a hemisphere. Label the four hemispheres pictured below.

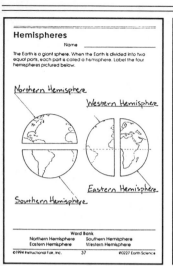

Northern Hemisphere
Western Hemisphere
Eastern Hemisphere
Southern Hemisphere

Word Bank

Northern Hemisphere	Southern Hemisphere
Eastern Hemisphere	Western Hemisphere

©1994 Instructional Fair, Inc.   37   #0227 Earth Science

More Than One Hemisphere

Name

You live in more than one hemisphere. Although it's impossible to live in the Northern and Southern Hemispheres, or the Eastern and Western Hemisphere at the same time, it is possible to live in the Northern and Eastern, or Northern and Western, or Southern and Eastern, or Southern and Western Hemisphere. Label the two hemispheres pictured in each hemisphere.

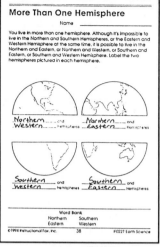

Northern and Western Hemispheres   Northern and Eastern Hemispheres

Southern and Western Hemispheres   Southern and Eastern Hemispheres

Word Bank

Northern	Southern
Eastern	Western

©1994 Instructional Fair, Inc.   38   #0227 Earth Science

Using Latitude and Longitude

Name

Use the latitude and longitude grid to pinpoint each location specified in the questions below.

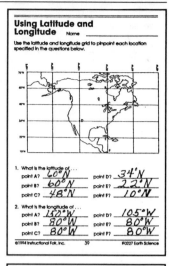

1. What is the latitude of . . .

point A?	60°N	point D?	34°N
point B?	60°N	point E?	22°N
point C?	48°N	point F?	10°N

2. What is the longitude of . . .

point A?	150°W	point D?	105°W
point B?	80°W	point E?	80°W
point C?	80°W	point F?	80°W

©1994 Instructional Fair, Inc.   39   #0227 Earth Science

Sea of Air

Name

Our atmosphere extends several hundred kilometers upward. In the illustration below notice different layers of the atmosphere and what may be found in those layers. Label each of the layers and objects found in these layers.

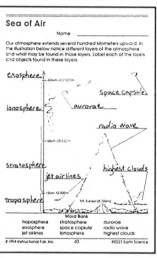

exosphere
space capsule
ionosphere
aurorae
radio wave
stratosphere
jet airlines
highest clouds
troposphere

Word Bank

troposphere	stratosphere	aurorae
exosphere	space capsule	radio wave
jet airlines	ionosphere	highest clouds

©1994 Instructional Fair, Inc.   40   #0227 Earth Science

The Center of the Earth

Name

The Earth has four layers. Color the layers of the Earth and the key.

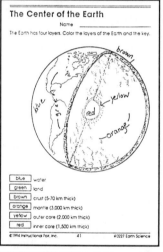

blue	water
green	land
brown	crust (5-70 km thick)
orange	mantle (3,000 km thick)
yellow	outer core (2,000 km thick)
red	inner core (1,500 km thick)

©1994 Instructional Fair, Inc.   41   #0227 Earth Science

Mohs Hardness Scale

Name

One of the most useful properties used for identification of a mineral is its hardness. The Mohs hardness scale measures a mineral's hardness by means of a simple scratch test. Name the mineral that belongs in each step of the Mohs Hardness Scale chart.

Mohs Hardness Scale		
Hardness	Mineral	Common Tests
1	Talc	Fingernail will scratch it.
2	Gypsum	
3	Calcite	Fingernail will not scratch it; a copper penny will.
4	Fluorite	Knife blade or window glass will scratch it.
5	Apatite	
6	Feldspar/Orthoclase	
7	Quartz	Will scratch a steel knife or window glass.
8	Topaz	
9	Corundum	
10	Diamond	Will scratch all common materials.

Word Bank

talc	diamond	fluorite
calcite	topaz	corundum
apatite	gypsum	quartz
feldspar/orthoclase		

©1994 Instructional Fair, Inc.   42   #0227 Earth Science

Classy Rocks

Name

There are three main groups of rock: igneous rock, metamorphic rock, and sedimentary rock. Each of the rocks pictured on this page belongs to one of these groups. In the space below each picture, tell to which group each rock belongs.

igneous   metamorphic   metamorphic
sedimentary   sedimentary   igneous
sedimentary   metamorphic   igneous
sedimentary

Kind of Rock	Definition
Igneous	cooled magma
Sedimentary	layers of loose material...
Metamorphic	rock that has been changed

Definitions

igneous	layers of loose material which solidified
metamorphic	cooled magma
sedimentary	rock that has been changed into a new rock

©1994 Instructional Fair, Inc.   43   #0227 Earth Science

Whose Fault Is It?

Name

A crack in the Earth's bedrock is called a fault. There are two types of faults, the strike-slip fault and the dip-slip fault.

Draw the San Andreas Fault line on the map of California, then label the two different kinds of faults.

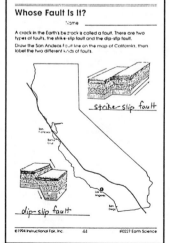

strike-slip fault

dip-slip fault

©1994 Instructional Fair, Inc.   44   #0227 Earth Science

Drifting Continents

Name

About 250 million years ago some say there was one continent called Pangaea (figure A). By 45 million years ago the land mass split into seven land masses (Figure B). Label the land masses in Figure B.

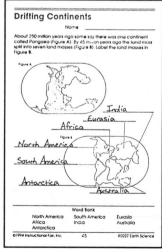

Figure A

Figure B

India
Eurasia
Africa
North America
South America
Antarctica
Australia

Word Bank

North America	South America	Eurasia
Africa	India	Australia
Antarctica		

©1994 Instructional Fair, Inc.   45   #0227 Earth Science

"Broken Plates"

Name _____

Below are puzzle pieces of the Earth's seven major plates. Cut out the plates and glue them together on a separate sheet of paper. Label the plates.

Word Bank

Pacific Plate	American Plate	Indo-Australian Plate
African Plate	Nazca Plate	
Antarctic Plate	Eurasian Plate	

©1994 Instructional Fair, Inc.   46   #0227 Earth Science

Earth's Moving Plates

Name _____

The Earth's crust is made of rigid plates that are always moving. The boundaries of some of these plates are along the edges of the continents, while others are in the middle of the ocean.

Using a source, label the eight plates pictured below.

Word Bank

Gorda Plate	North American Plate	Cocos Plate
Pacific Plate	South American Plate	Nazca Plate
Antarctic Plate	Caribbean Plate	

©1994 Instructional Fair, Inc.   47   #0227 Earth Science

Volcanoes

Name _____

Label the parts of this volcano.

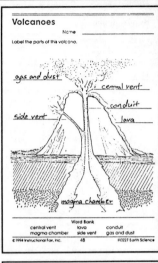

Word Bank

central vent	lava	conduit
magma chamber	side vent	gas and dust

©1994 Instructional Fair, Inc.   48   #0227 Earth Science

"Ring of Fire"

Name _____

There are more than 500 active volcanoes in the world. More than half of these encircle the Pacific Ocean in an area called the "Ring of Fire." Research the "Ring of Fire." Color the region, locate and label some of its well-known volcanoes.

Suggested answers.

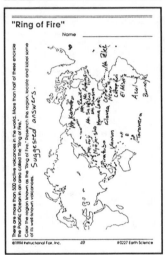

©1994 Instructional Fair, Inc.   49   #0227 Earth Science

Forming Igneous Rock

Name _____

Igneous rock is one of the three major types of rock. It is formed by the hardening of molten rock (magma). Magma does not always reach the earth's surface as erupting lava. It often forms other igneous rock structures underground.

Label the igneous rock structures shown here.

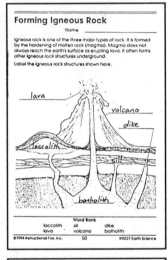

Word Bank

laccolith	sill	volcano	dike
lava	volcano	batholith

©1994 Instructional Fair, Inc.   50   #0227 Earth Science

Drilling for Oil

Name _____

Most oil is found thousands of feet beneath the surface of the earth. It is trapped beneath layers of nonporous rock, such as shale, which will not allow the oil to pass through. Often pockets of natural gas will form where there is oil. Oil companies drill for oil using large drills that grind through the ground and rock.

The illustration below shows an example of where oil can be found. Label the illustration.

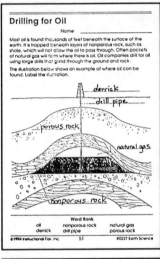

Word Bank

oil	nonporous rock	natural gas
derrick	drill pipe	porous rock

©1994 Instructional Fair, Inc.   51   #0227 Earth Science

Coral Reefs

Name _____

Three types of coral reefs are pictured below.

1. Label each type of coral reef.
2. Label the features that are enclosed by the reef.
3. Number the steps in the formation of an atoll.

atoll
lagoon
Step No. _3_

fringing reef
inactive volcano
Step No. _1_

barrier reef
island
Step No. _2_

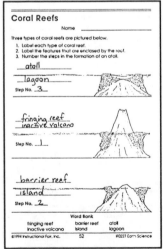

Word Bank

fringing reef	barrier reef	atoll
inactive volcano	island	lagoon

©1994 Instructional Fair, Inc.   52   #0227 Earth Science

Groundwater at Work

Name _____

Groundwater is water in the ground that is near the surface. People remove it with wells. Label the pictures below.

sinkhole
stalactite
stalagmite
cave
aquifer
artesian well

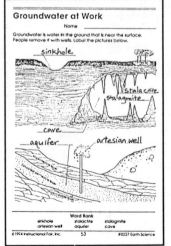

Word Bank

sinkhole	stalactite	stalagmite
artesian well	aquifer	cave

©1994 Instructional Fair, Inc.   53   #0227 Earth Science

Ocean Currents

Name _____

Water moves within the oceans in streams called currents. Label the ocean currents pictured.

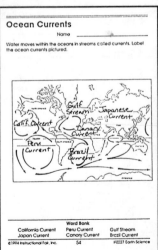

Word Bank

California Current	Peru Current	Gulf Stream
Japan Current	Canary Current	Brazil Current

©1994 Instructional Fair, Inc.   54   #0227 Earth Science

Landform Regions of the United States

Name _____

The continental United States can be divided into several major landform regions. Label each region.

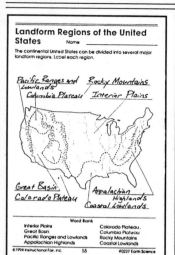

Pacific Ranges and Lowlands
Columbia Plateau
Rocky Mountains
Interior Plains
Great Basin
Colorado Plateau
Appalachian Highlands
Coastal Lowlands

Word Bank

Interior Plains	Colorado Plateau
Great Basin	Columbia Plateau
Pacific Ranges and Lowlands	Rocky Mountains
Appalachian Highlands	Coastal Lowlands

©1994 Instructional Fair, Inc.   55   #0227 Earth Science

Topographic Maps

Name _____

A topographic map uses contour lines to show the elevation and slope of hills, valleys, and other natural features. Label the various land features and elements of the topographic map pictured.

mountain-top
index contour line
gentle slope
contour line
steep slope
river

Word Bank

contour line	index contour line	mountain top
steep slope	gentle slope	river

©1994 Instructional Fair, Inc.   56   #0227 Earth Science

Topographical Maps

Name _____

Topographical maps give the geographical positions and elevations of both manmade and natural features. Using the contour lines and contour intervals, label the elevations of the features on this map.

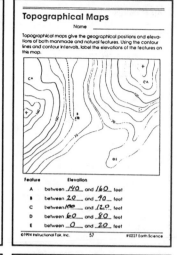

Feature	Elevation
A	between *140* and *160* feet
B	between *20* and *40* feet
C	between *100* and *120* feet
D	between *60* and *80* feet
E	between *0* and *20* feet

©1994 Instructional Fair, Inc.   57   #0227 Earth Science

Meandering River

Name _____

A river goes through different stages of development as it erodes its channel. Label the parts of the river.

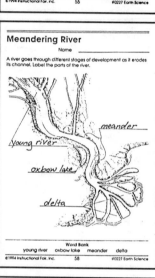

meander
young river
oxbow lake
delta

Word Bank

young river	oxbow lake	meander	delta

©1994 Instructional Fair, Inc.   58   #0227 Earth Science

River System

Name _____

A river may begin its journey to the sea high up in the mountains as a melting glacier, or as a number of small streams and brooks high up in hills. As the river flows downhill the moving water reshapes the land. The river and all the water that flows into it make up the river system.

Label the parts of the river system.

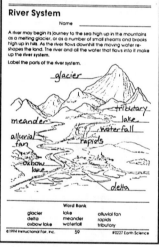

glacier
tributary
meander
lake
waterfall
alluvial fan
rapids
oxbow lake
delta

Word Bank

glacier	lake	alluvial fan
delta	meander	rapids
oxbow lake	waterfall	tributary

©1994 Instructional Fair, Inc.   59   #0227 Earth Science

Glaciers

Name _____

Tons of ice and trapped rock scrape mountain walls as a glacier creeps down a mountain. The tremendous force of the moving glacier reshapes the mountain slopes in its path, leaving behind deposits of rock.

Label the formations made by the moving glacier.

cirque
kettle lake
crevasses
drumlin
esker
terminal moraine

Word Bank

esker	drumlin	kettle lake
terminal moraine	crevasses	cirque

©1994 Instructional Fair, Inc.   60   #0227 Earth Science

Weather Map Symbols

Name _____

Weather maps, like the one on this page, provide data from which meteorologists prepare weather forecasts. To accurately read a weather map you must be able to understand the weather map symbols.

Label each of these symbols.

cold front
snow
occluded front
cloudy
stationary front
high pressure
Clear skies
low pressure
rain
wind speed and direction
partly cloudy
thunderstorm

Word Bank

rain	partly cloudy	clear skies
occluded front	warm front	cold front
high pressure	thunderstorm	cloudy
wind speed and direction	low pressure	
stationary front		

©1994 Instructional Fair, Inc.   61   #0227 Earth Science

Precipitation

Name _____

Precipitation is water vapor that condenses and falls to the earth. Depending on the conditions in the atmosphere, precipitation can fall in a number of forms.

Identify each form of precipitation by drawing its symbol next to its description.

Symbols		Symbol	Definition
rain	•••	≡	Clouds that form close to the ground.
drizzle		△	Droplets that freeze as they get closer to the ground.
rain showers	◦	,	Light mist of droplets falling to the earth.
sleet	△	▲	Droplets of water freeze around ice crystals as they bounce up and down within a storm cloud. Fall to earth when they get heavy.
snow	✳	✳	Vapor that changes directly into crystalline flakes because of freezing temperatures.
hail	▲	••••	Water vapor that forms droplets and falls to the earth.
fog	≡	◦	Large amount of droplets falling to the earth.

©1994 Instructional Fair, Inc.   62   #0227 Earth Science

Relative Humidity

Name _____

Relative humidity is the amount of water vapor that the air can hold at a certain temperature. Relative humidity is measured with a hygrometer.

Use the table to find the relative humidity for the data recorded on the chart below.

Day	Dry Temp.	Wet Temp.	Relative Humidity
Mon.	22°	21°	*92%*
Tues.	23°	21°	*84%*
Wed.	21°	19°	*83%*
Thurs.	19°	18°	*91%*
Fri.	18°	15°	*73%*
Sat.	19°	15°	*65%*
Sun.	17°	13°	*64%*

Dry bulb temp. C°	Difference between wet and dry temperatures							
	1°	2°	3°	4°	5°	6°	7°	8°
15°	90	83	71	61	53	44	36	27
16°	90	81	71	63	54	46	38	30
17°	90	81	72	54	55	47	40	32
18°	91	82	73	65	57	49	41	34
19°	91	82	74	65	58	50	43	36
20°	91	83	74	66	59	51	44	37
21°	91	83	75	67	60	53	46	39
22°	92	83	76	68	61	54	47	40
23°	92	84	76	69	62	55	48	42
24°	92	84	77	69	62	56	49	43
25°	92	84	77	70	63	57	50	44
26°	92	85	78	71	64	58	51	46
27°	92	85	78	71	65	58	52	47

Use your data to make a graph of the relative humidity.

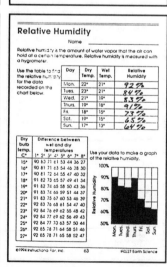

©1994 Instructional Fair, Inc.   63   #0227 Earth Science

©1994 Instructional Fair, Inc.   IF0227 Earth Science

Air Currents

Name _____

Name the three air current phenomena pictured below using the Word Bank. Then fill in each explanation.

This picture shows: the Coriolis effect

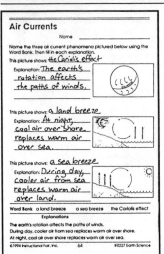

Explanation: The earth's rotation affects the paths of winds.

This picture shows: a land breeze

Explanation: At night, cool air over shore replaces warm air over sea.

This picture shows: a sea breeze

Explanation: During day, cooler air from sea replaces warm air over land.

Word Bank   a land breeze   a sea breeze   the Coriolis effect

Explanations

The earth's rotation affects the paths of winds.
During day, cooler air from sea replaces warm air over shore.
At night, cool air over shore replaces warm air over sea.

The Water Cycle

Name _____

The never-ending circulation of the waters of the earth from the oceans, to the air, and to the land is called the water cycle. Label the three major steps in the water cycle below. Then explain how the water cycle works in your own words.

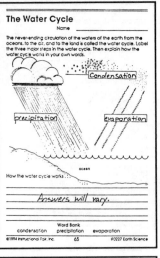

Condensation

precipitation

evaporation

ocean

How the water cycle works:

Answers will vary.

Word Bank
condensation   precipitation   evaporation

What's Up Front?

Name _____

A front is where two air masses meet. Changes in the weather take place along a front.

Label the two fronts and the kinds of air masses in the spaces and arrows below.

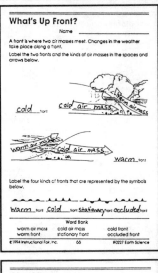

warm air mass

cold   cold air mass

front

warm air mass   cold air mass

warm   front

Label the four kinds of fronts that are represented by the symbols below.

warm front   cold front   stationary front   occluded front

Word Bank
warm air mass   cold air mass   cold front
warm front   stationary front   occluded front

A Cold Front

Name _____

The illustration below is a front between two air masses. The cooler air mass is replacing the warmer air mass.

Label the cloud types associated with this cold front.

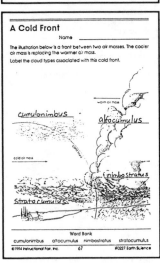

warm air mass

cumulonimbus

altocumulus

cold air mass

nimbostratus

Stratocumulus

Word Bank
cumulonimbus   altocumulus   nimbostratus   stratocumulus

A Warm Front

Name _____

The illustration below is a front between two air masses. A warm air mass is pushing a cold air mass.

Label the cloud types associated with the warm front pictured.

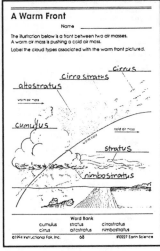

cirrus

Cirro stratus

altostratus

warm air mass

cumulus

cold air mass

stratus

nimbostratus

Word Bank
cumulus   stratus   cirrostratus
cirrus   altostratus   nimbostratus

Cloud Types

Name _____

Label the cloud types pictured below.

cirrus

cirrostratus

cirrocumulus

alto stratus

altocumulus

cumulonimbus

Stratocumulus

cumulus   nimbostratus

stratus

Word Bank
stratus   cumulus   cirrus
altostratus   altocumulus   cirrocumulus
cirrostratus   cumulonimbus   nimbostratus
stratocumulus

Clouds and Weather

Name _____

Different types of clouds are associated with a specific kind of weather. Four kinds of clouds are pictured below. Write the name of the cloud type, a description of the cloud, and the weather associated with each.

Cloud Type	Name	Description	Associated Weather
	cumulus	piles of "puffy" Clouds	fair, sometimes showers
	cumulo-nimbus	tall, dark and billowing	thunderstorms
	stratus	smooth sheets or layers	steady drizzle
	cirrus	thin, wispy clouds	fair

Word Bank
thunderstorms   cumulonimbus   cumulus
fair, sometimes showers   thin, wispy clouds   stratus
steady drizzle   tall, dark and billowing   fair
smooth sheets, or layers   piles of "puffy" clouds   cirrus

Tomorrow's Weather Forecast

Name _____

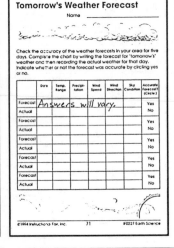

Check the accuracy of the weather forecasts in your area for five days. Complete the chart by writing the forecast for "tomorrow's" weather and then recording the actual weather for that day. Indicate whether or not the forecast was accurate by circling yes or no.

	Date	Temp. Range	Precipi-tation	Wind Speed	Wind Direction	Sky Condition	Accurate Forecast? (Circle)
Forecast							Yes
Actual							No
Forecast							Yes
Actual							No
Forecast							Yes
Actual							No
Forecast							Yes
Actual							No
Forecast							Yes
Actual							No

Answers will vary.

Weather Instruments

Name _____

Meteorologists use a variety of instruments to gather data. Many of these instruments are pictured. Identify each instrument and tell what it measures.

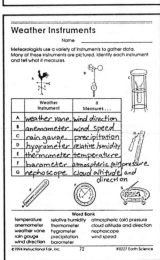

	Weather Instrument	Measures...
A	weather vane	wind direction
B	anemometer	wind speed
C	rain gauge	precipitation
D	hygrometer	relative humidity
E	thermometer	temperature
F	barometer	atmospheric (air) pressure
G	nephoscope	cloud altitude and direction

Word Bank
temperature   relative humidity   atmospheric (air) pressure
anemometer   thermometer   cloud altitude and direction
weather vane   hygrometer   nephoscope
rain gauge   precipitation   wind speed
wind direction   barometer

Hemispheres

Name _____

The Earth is a giant sphere. When the Earth is divided into two equal parts, each part is called a hemisphere. Label the four hemispheres pictured below.

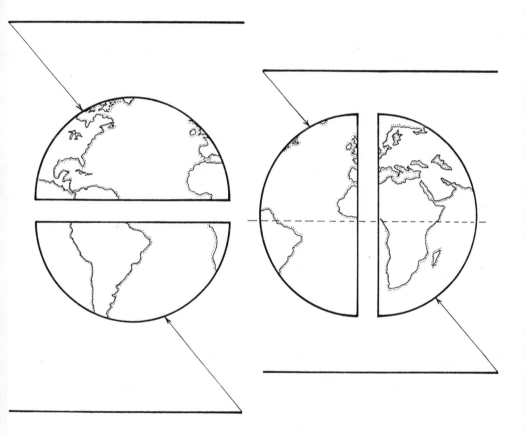

More Than One Hemisphere

Name _____

You live in more than one hemisphere. Although it's impossible to live in the Northern and Southern Hemispheres, or the Eastern and Western Hemisphere at the same time, it is possible to live in the Northern and Eastern, or Northern and Western, or Southern and Eastern, or Southern and Western Hemisphere. Label the two hemispheres pictured in each hemisphere.

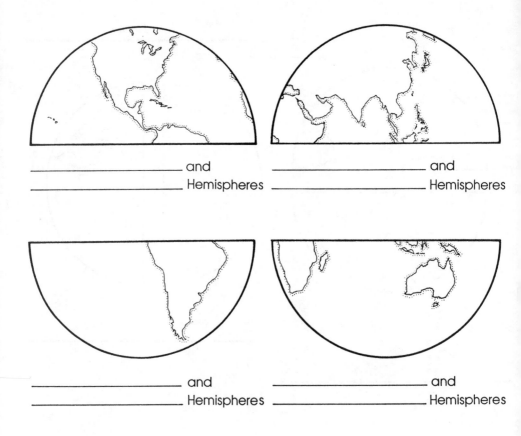

_____ and
_____ Hemispheres

_____ and
_____ Hemispheres

_____ and
_____ Hemispheres

_____ and
_____ Hemispheres

Word Bank

Northern   Southern
Eastern   Western

Using Latitude and Longitude

Name _____

Use the latitude and longitude grid to pinpoint each location specified in the questions below.

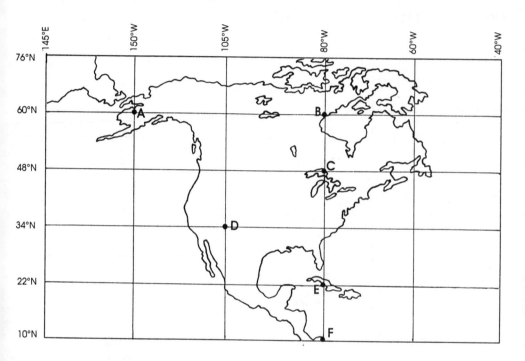

1. What is the latitude of . . .

   point **A**? _____   point **D**? _____

   point **B**? _____   point **E**? _____

   point **C**? _____   point **F**? _____

2. What is the longitude of . . .

   point **A**? _____   point **D**? _____

   point **B**? _____   point **E**? _____

   point **C**? _____   point **F**? _____

Sea of Air

Name _____

Our atmosphere extends several hundred kilometers upward. In the illustration below notice different layers of the atmosphere and what may be found in those layers. Label each of the layers and objects found in these layers.

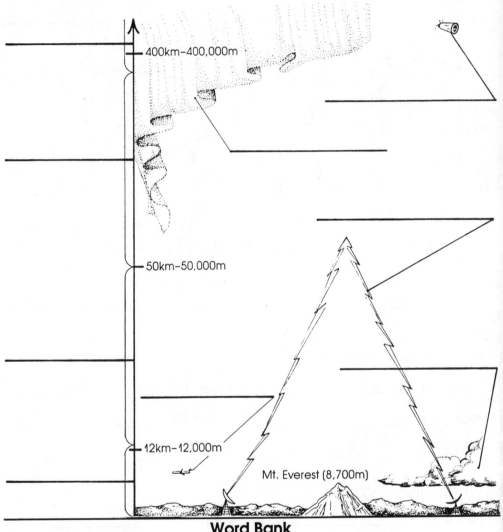

400km–400,000m

50km–50,000m

12km–12,000m

Mt. Everest (8,700m)

Word Bank

troposphere	stratosphere	aurorae
exosphere	space capsule	radio wave
jet airlines	ionosphere	highest clouds

The Center of the Earth

Name _____

The Earth has four layers. Color the layers of the Earth and the key.

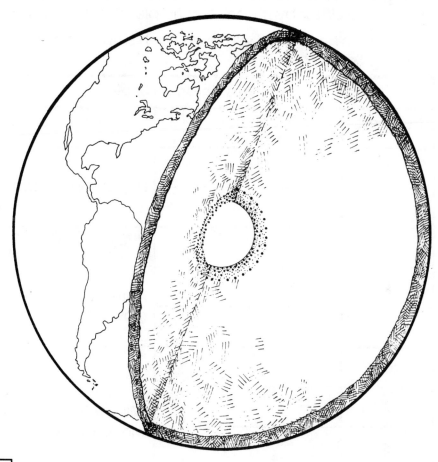

blue	water
green	land
brown	crust (5-70 km thick)
orange	mantle (3,000 km thick)
yellow	outer core (2,000 km thick)
red	inner core (1,500 km thick)

Mohs Hardness Scale

Name _____

One of the most useful properties used for identification of a mineral is its hardness. The Mohs hardness scale measures a mineral's hardness by means of a simple scratch test.

Name the mineral that belongs in each step of the Mohs Hardness Scale chart.

Mohs Hardness Scale		
Hardness	**Mineral**	**Common Tests**
1		Fingernail will scratch it.
2		
3		Fingernail will not scratch it; a copper penny will.
4		Knife blade or window glass will scratch it.
5		
6		Will scratch a steel knife or window glass.
7		
8		
9		
10		Will scratch all common materials.

Word Bank

talc   diamond   fluorite
calcite   topaz   corundum
apatite   gypsum   quartz
feldspar/orthoclase

Classy Rocks

Name _____

There are three main groups of rock: **igneous** rock, **metamorphic** rock, and **sedimentary** rock. Each of the rocks pictured on this page belongs to one of these groups. Fill in the definitions. In the space below each picture, tell to which group each rock belongs.

granite

gneiss

marble

limestone

shale

basalt

sandstone

slate

obsidian

conglomerate

Kind of Rock	Definition
Igneous	
Sedimentary	
Metamorphic	

Word Bank	Definitions
igneous metamorphic sedimentary	layers of loose material which solidified cooled magma rock that has been changed into a new rock

Whose Fault Is It?

Name _____

A crack in the Earth's bedrock is called a fault. There are two types of faults, the **strike-slip fault** and the **dip-slip fault**.

Draw the San Andreas Fault line on the map of California, then label the two different kinds of faults.

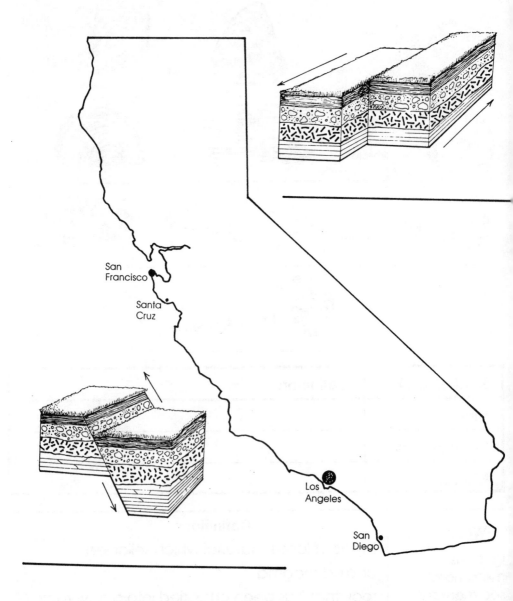

Drifting Continents

Name _____

About 250 million years ago some say there was one continent called Pangaea (Figure **A**). By 45 million years ago the land mass split into seven land masses (Figure **B**). Label the land masses in Figure **B**.

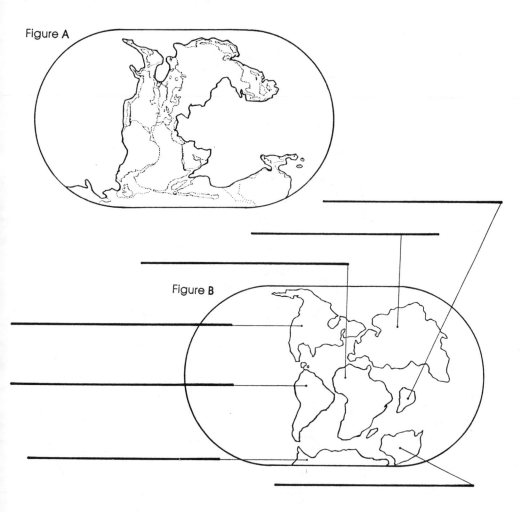

Figure A

Figure B

Word Bank

North America	South America	Eurasia
Africa	India	Australia
Antarctica		

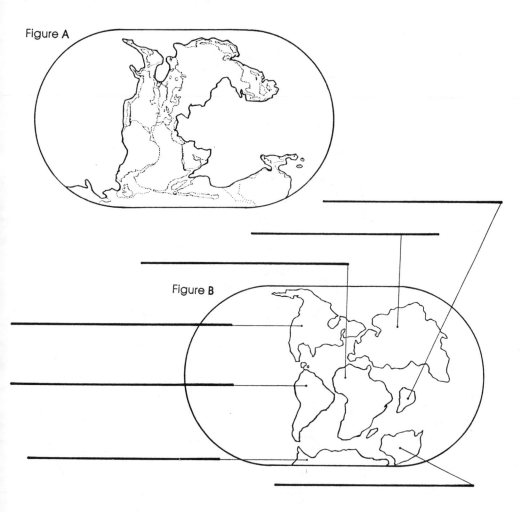

"Broken Plates"

Name _____

Below are puzzle pieces of the Earth's seven major plates. Cut out the plates and glue them together on a separate sheet of paper. Label the plates.

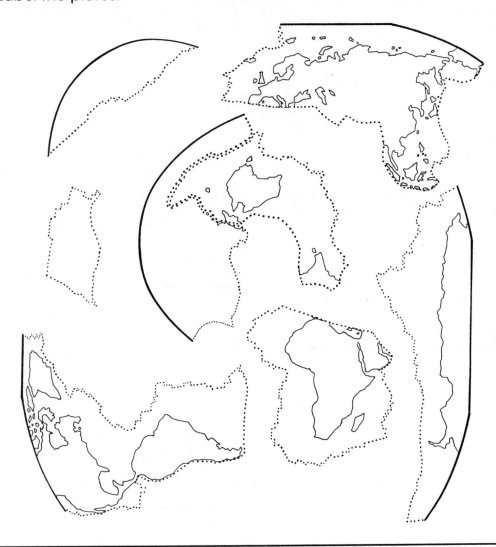

Word Bank

Pacific Plate   American Plate   Indo-Australian Plate
African Plate   Nazca Plate
Antarctic Plate   Eurasian Plate

Earth's Moving Plates

Name _____

The Earth's crust is made of rigid plates that are always moving. The boundaries of some of these plates are along the edges of the continents, while others are in the middle of the ocean.

Using a source, label the eight plates pictured below.

Word Bank

Gorda Plate	North American Plate	Cocos Plate
Pacific Plate	South American Plate	Nazca Plate
Antarctic Plate	Caribbean Plate	

Volcanoes

Name _____

Label the parts of this volcano.

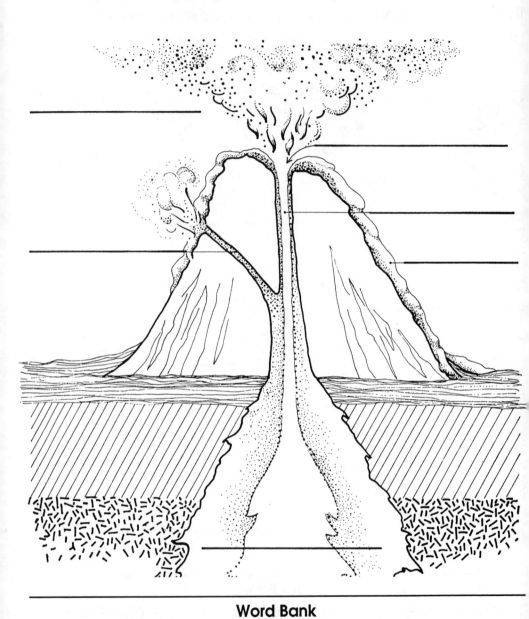

Word Bank

| central vent | lava | conduit |
| magma chamber | side vent | gas and dust |

"Ring of Fire"

Name _____

There are more than 500 active volcanoes in the world. More than half of these encircle the Pacific Ocean in an area called the "Ring of Fire."

Color the region known as the "Ring of Fire." Research this region, locate and label some of its well-known volcanoes.

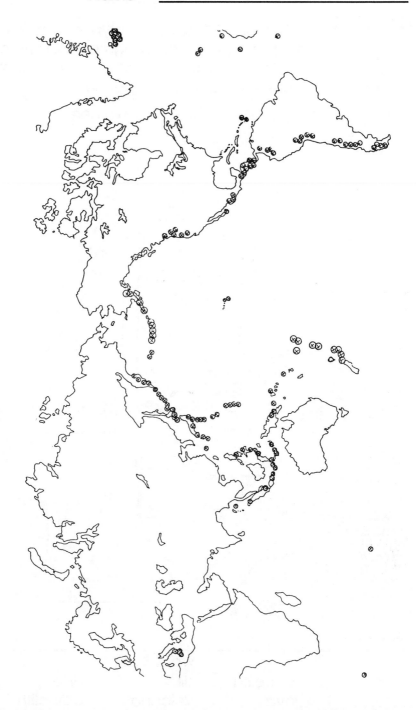

Forming Igneous Rock

Name _____

Igneous rock is one of the three major types of rock. It is formed by the hardening of molten rock (magma). Magma does not always reach the earth's surface as erupting lava. It often forms other igneous rock structures underground.

Label the igneous rock structures shown here.

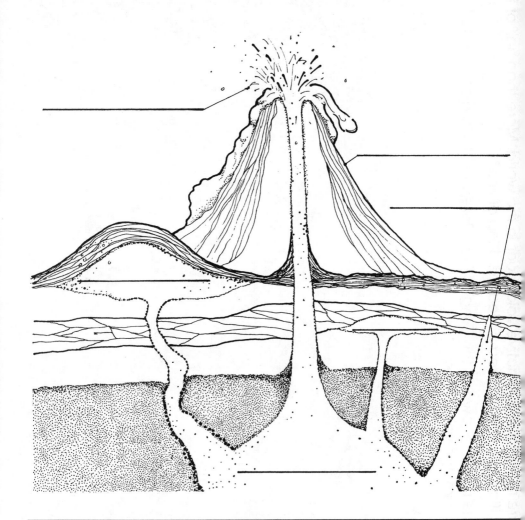

Word Bank

laccolith	sill	dike
lava	volcano	batholith

Drilling for Oil

Name _____

Most oil is found thousands of feet beneath the surface of the earth. It is trapped beneath layers of nonporous rock, such as shale, which will not allow the oil to pass through. Often pockets of natural gas will form where there is oil. Oil companies drill for oil using large drills that grind through the ground and rock.

The illustration below shows an example of where oil can be found. Label the illustration.

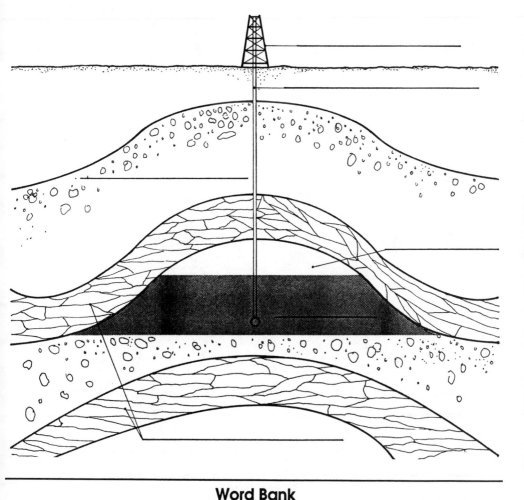

Word Bank

oil	nonporous rock	natural gas
derrick	drill pipe	porous rock

Coral Reefs

Name _____

Three types of coral reefs are pictured below.

1. Label each type of coral reef.
2. Label the features that are enclosed by the reef.
3. Number the steps in the formation of an atoll.

_____

_____

Step No. _____

_____

_____

Step No. _____

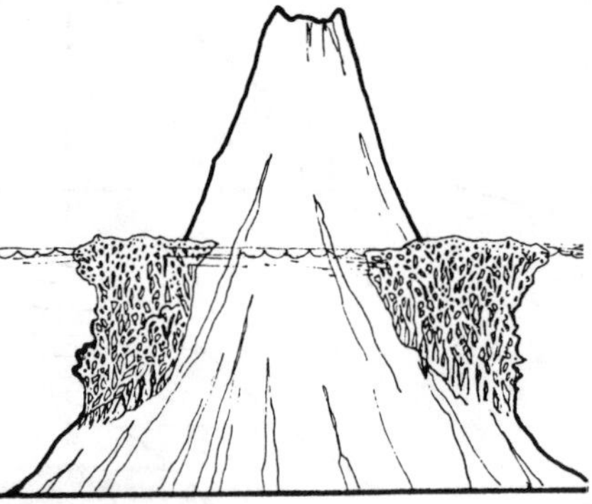

_____

_____

Step No. _____

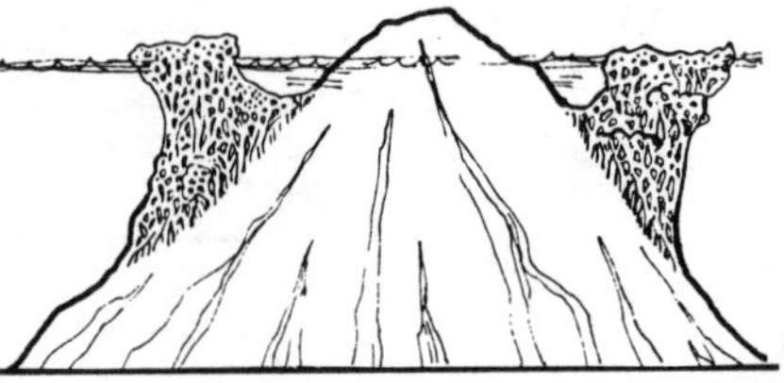

Word Bank

fringing reef	barrier reef	atoll
inactive volcano	island	lagoon

Groundwater at Work

Name _____

Groundwater is water in the ground that is near the surface.
People remove it with wells. Label the pictures below.

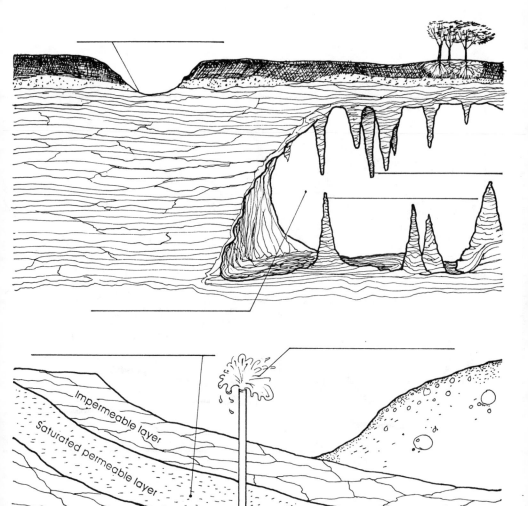

Word Bank

sinkhole	stalactite	stalagmite
artesian well	aquifer	cave

Ocean Currents

Name _____

Water moves within the oceans in streams called currents. Label the ocean currents pictured.

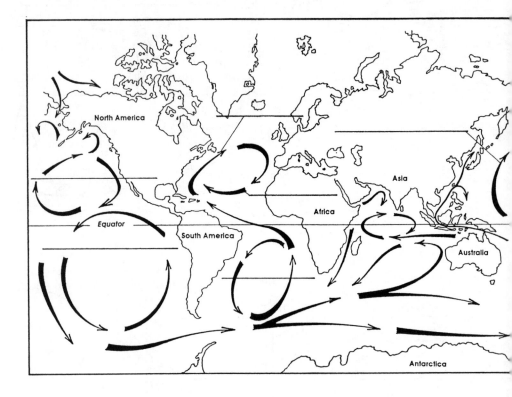

Word Bank

California Current	Peru Current	Gulf Stream
Japan Current	Canary Current	Brazil Current

Landform Regions of the United States

Name _____

The continental United States can be divided into several major landform regions. Label each region.

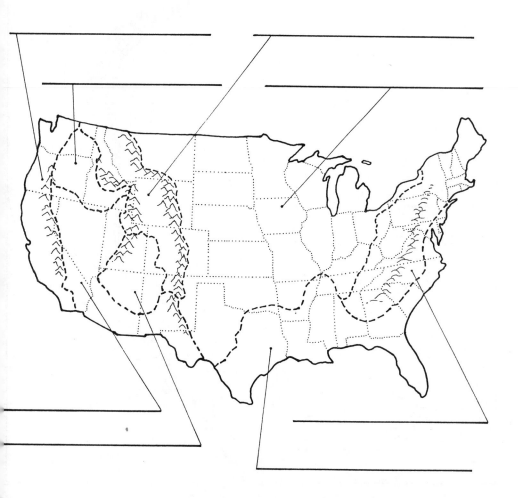

Word Bank

Interior Plains

Great Basin

Pacific Ranges and Lowlands

Appalachian Highlands

Colorado Plateau

Columbia Plateau

Rocky Mountains

Coastal Lowlands

Topographic Maps

Name _____

A topographic map uses contour lines to show the elevation and slope of hills, valleys, and other natural features. Label the various land features and elements of the topographic map pictured.

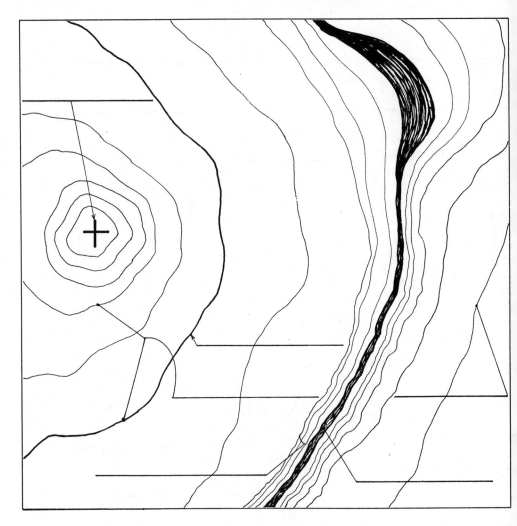

Word Bank

contour line	index contour line	mountain top
steep slope	gentle slope	river

   IF0227 Earth Science

Topographical Maps

Name _____

Topographical maps give the geographical positions and elevations of both manmade and natural features. Using the contour lines and contour intervals, label the elevations of the features on this map.

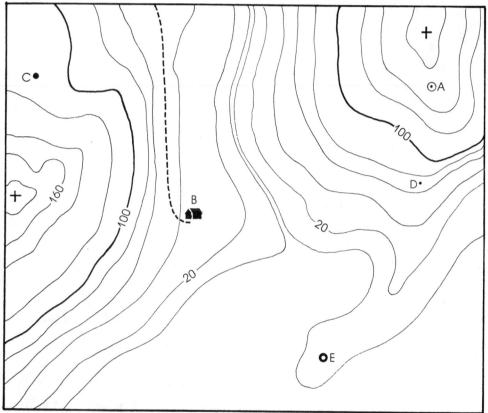

Feature   **Elevation**

A   between _____ and _____ feet

B   between _____ and _____ feet

C   between _____ and _____ feet

D   between _____ and _____ feet

E   between _____ and _____ feet

Meandering River

Name _____

A river goes through different stages of development as it erodes
its channel. Label the parts of the river.

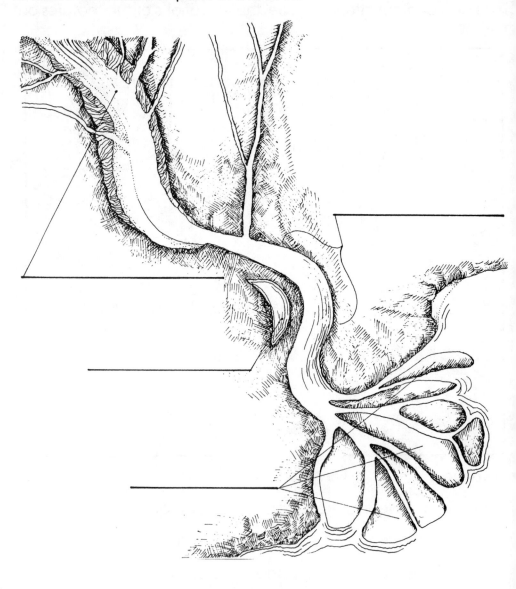

Word Bank

young river   oxbow lake   meander   delta

River System

Name _____

A river may begin its journey to the sea high up in the mountains as a melting glacier, or as a number of small streams and brooks high up in hills. As the river flows downhill the moving water re-shapes the land. The river and all the water that flows into it make up the **river system**.

Label the parts of the river system.

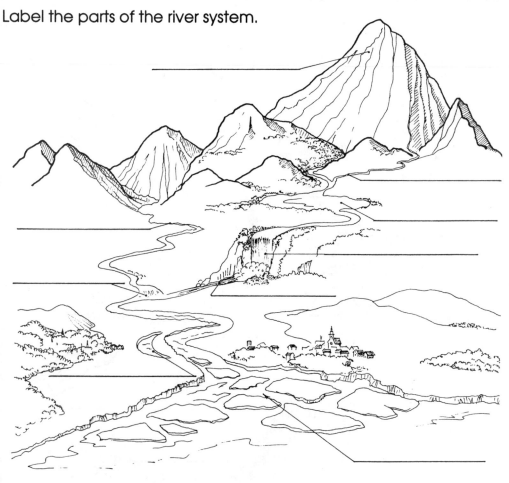

Word Bank

glacier	lake	alluvial fan
delta	meander	rapids
oxbow lake	waterfall	tributary

Glaciers

Name _____

Tons of ice and trapped rock scrape mountain walls as a glacier creeps down a mountain. The tremendous force of the moving glacier reshapes the mountain slopes in its path, leaving behind deposits of rock.

Label the formations made by the moving glacier.

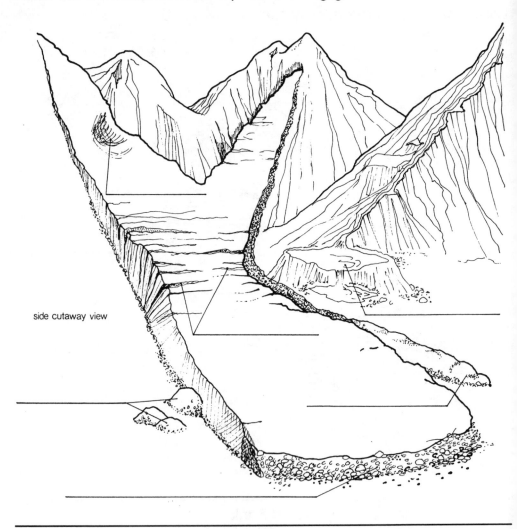

side cutaway view

Word Bank

esker	drumlin	kettle lake
terminal moraine	crevasses	cirque

Weather Map Symbols

Name _____

Weather maps, like the one on this page, provide data from which meteorologists prepare weather forecasts. To accurately read a weather map you must be able to understand the weather map symbols.

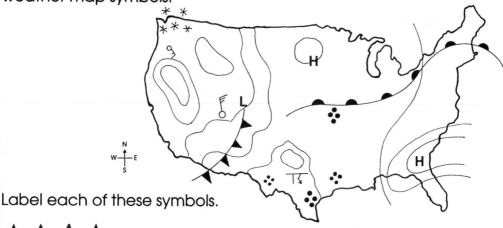

Label each of these symbols.

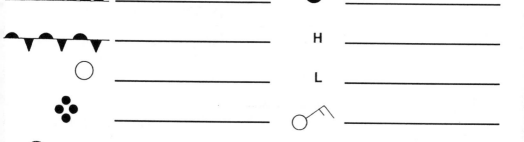

Word Bank

rain	partly cloudy	clear skies
occluded front	warm front	cold front
high pressure	thunderstorm	cloudy
wind speed and direction	low pressure	snow
stationary front		

Precipitation

Name _____

Precipitation is water vapor that condenses and falls to the earth. Depending on the conditions in the atmosphere, precipitation can fall in a number of forms.

Identify each form of precipitation by drawing its symbol next to its description.

Symbols

rain

drizzle

rain showers

sleet

snow

hail

fog

Symbol	Definition
	Clouds that form close to the ground.
	Droplets that freeze as they get closer to the ground.
	Light mist of droplets falling to the earth.
	Droplets of water freeze around ice crystals as they bounce up and down within a storm cloud. Fall to earth when they get heavy.
	Vapor that changes directly into crystalline flakes because of freezing temperatures.
	Water vapor that forms droplets and falls to the earth.
	Large amount of droplets falling to the earth.

Relative Humidity

Name _____

Relative humidity is the amount of water vapor that the air can hold at a certain temperature. Relative humidity is measured with a hygrometer.

Use the table to find the relative humidity for the data recorded on the chart below.

Day	Dry Temp.	Wet Temp.	Relative Humidity
Mon.	22°	21°	
Tues.	23°	21°	
Wed.	21°	19°	
Thurs.	19°	18°	
Fri.	18°	15°	
Sat.	19°	15°	
Sun.	17°	13°	

Dry bulb temp. C°	Difference between wet and dry temperatures							
	1°	2°	3°	4°	5°	6°	7°	8°
15°	90	80	71	61	53	44	36	27
16°	90	81	71	63	54	46	38	30
17°	90	81	72	64	55	47	40	32
18°	91	82	73	65	57	49	41	34
19°	91	82	74	65	58	50	43	36
20°	91	83	74	66	59	51	44	37
21°	91	83	75	67	60	53	46	39
22°	92	83	76	68	61	54	47	40
23°	92	84	76	69	62	55	48	42
24°	92	84	77	69	62	56	49	43
25°	92	84	77	70	63	57	50	44
26°	92	85	78	71	64	58	51	46
27°	92	85	78	71	65	58	52	47

Use your data to make a graph of the relative humidity.

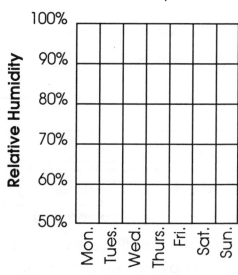

Air Currents

Name _____

Name the three air current phenomena pictured below using the Word Bank. Then fill in each explanation.

This picture shows: _____

    Explanation: _____

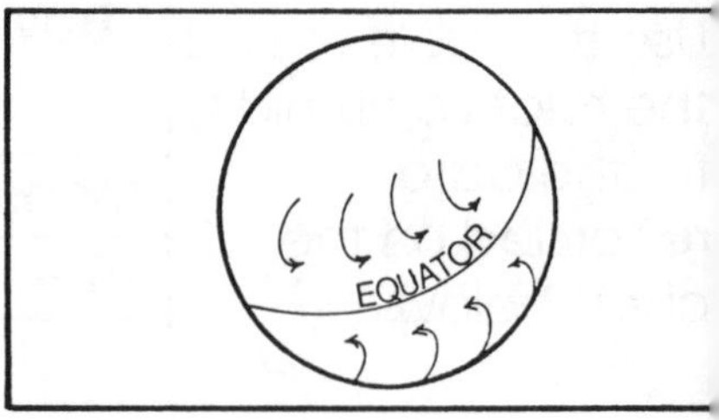

_____

_____

_____

This picture shows: _____

    Explanation: _____

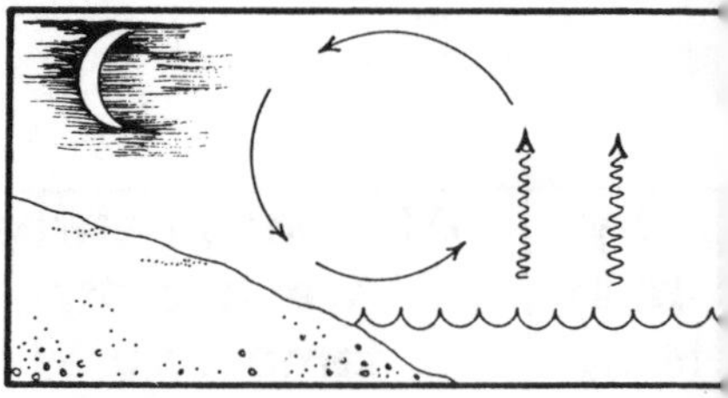

_____

_____

_____

This picture shows: _____

    Explanation: _____

_____

_____

_____

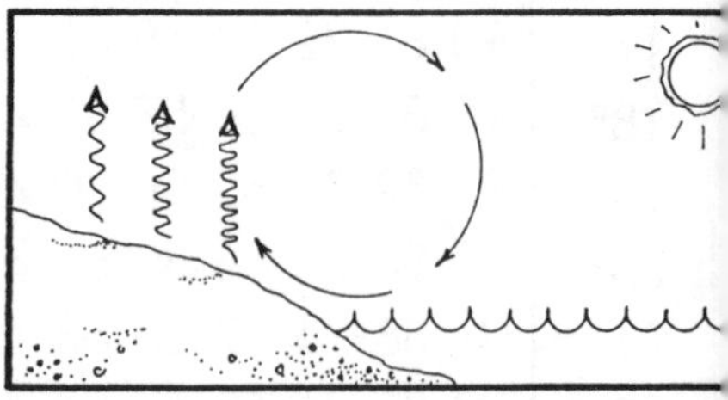

Word Bank   a land breeze   a sea breeze   the Coriolis effect

Explanations

The earth's rotation affects the paths of winds.

During day, cooler air from sea replaces warm air over shore.

At night, cool air over shore replaces warm air over sea.

The Water Cycle

Name _____

The never-ending circulation of the waters of the earth from the oceans, to the air, and to the land is called the water cycle. Label the three major steps in the water cycle. Then explain how the water cycle works in your own words.

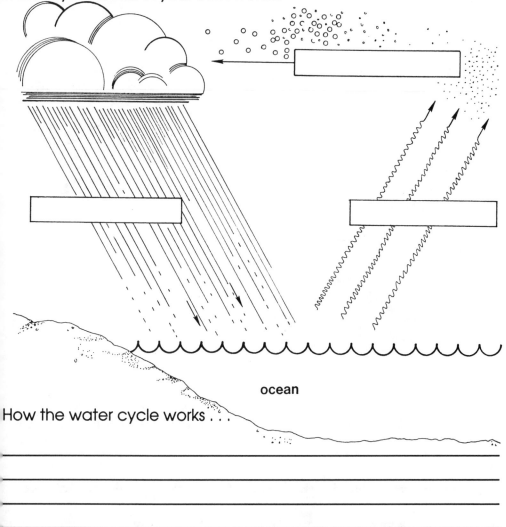

ocean

How the water cycle works . . .

_____
_____
_____
_____
_____
_____

Word Bank

condensation   precipitation   evaporation

What's Up Front?

Name _____

A front is where two air masses meet. Changes in the weather take place along a front.

Label the two fronts and the kinds of air masses in the spaces and arrows below.

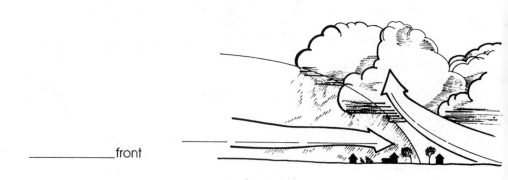

_____front

_____front

Label the four kinds of fronts that are represented by the symbols below.

_____front   _____front   _____front   _____front

Word Bank

warm air mass	cold air mass	cold front
warm front	stationary front	occluded front

A Cold Front

Name _____

The illustration below is a front between two air masses. The cooler air mass is replacing the warmer air mass.

Label the cloud types associated with this cold front.

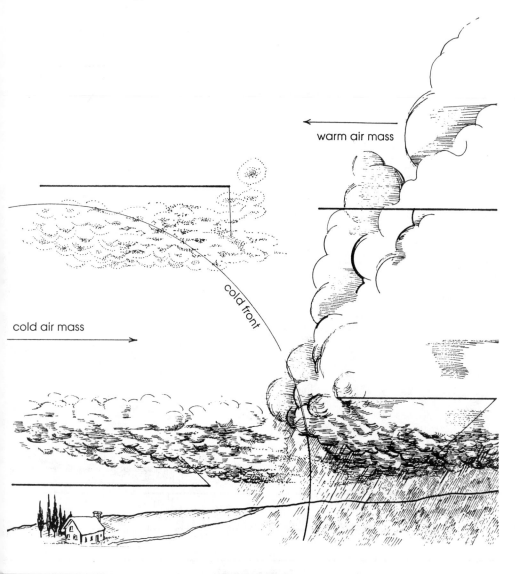

Word Bank

cumulonimbus   altocumulus   nimbostratus   stratocumulus

A Warm Front

Name _____

The illustration below is a front between two air masses.
A warm air mass is pushing a cold air mass.

Label the cloud types associated with the warm front pictured.

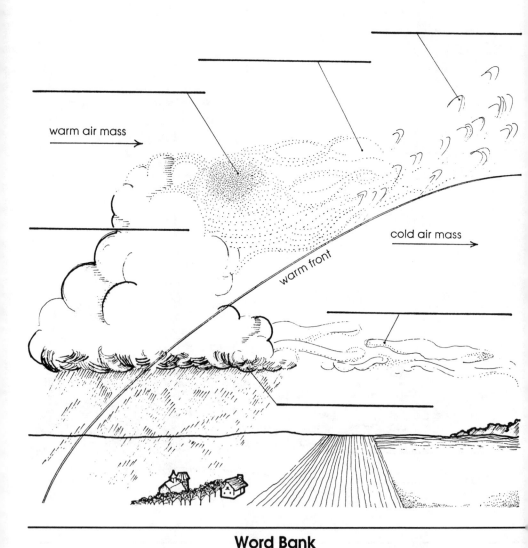

Word Bank

cumulus	stratus	cirrostratus
cirrus	altostratus	nimbostratus

Cloud Types

Name _____

Label the cloud types pictured below.

Word Bank

stratus   cumulus   cirrus

altostratus   altocumulus   cirrocumulus

cirrostratus   cumulonimbus   nimbostratus

stratocumulus

Clouds and Weather

Name _____

Different types of clouds are associated with a specific kind of weather. Four kinds of clouds are pictured below. Write the name of the cloud type, a description of the cloud, and the weather associated with each.

Cloud Type	Name	Description	Associated Weather

Word Bank

thunderstorms	cumulonimbus	cumulus
fair, sometimes showers	thin, wispy clouds	stratus
steady drizzle	tall, dark and billowing	fair
smooth sheets, or layers	piles of "puffy" clouds	cirrus

Tomorrow's Weather Forecast

Name _____

Check the accuracy of the weather forecasts in your area for five days. Complete the chart by writing the forecast for "tomorrow's" weather and then recording the actual weather for that day. Indicate whether or not the forecast was accurate by circling yes or no.

	Date	Temp. Range	Precipi-tation	Wind Speed	Wind Direction	Sky Condition	Accurate Forecast? (Circle.)
Forecast							Yes
Actual							No
Forecast							Yes
Actual							No
Forecast							Yes
Actual							No
Forecast							Yes
Actual							No
Forecast							Yes
Actual							No

Weather Instruments

Name _____

Meteorologists use a variety of instruments to gather data. Many of these instruments are pictured. Identify each instrument and tell what it measures.

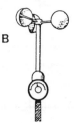

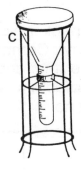

	Weather Instrument	It Measures . . .
A		
B		
C		
D		
E		
F		
G		

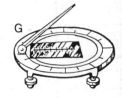

Word Bank

temperature   relative humidity   atmospheric (air) pressure
anemometer   thermometer   cloud altitude and direction
weather vane   hygrometer   nephoscope
rain gauge   precipitation   wind speed
wind direction   barometer